PENGUIN BOOKS

LANGUAGE MYTHS

Laurie Bauer is Reader in Linguistics at Victoria University of Wellington, New Zealand. He is the author of many books and articles on word-formation, international varieties of English and language change in current English, including *Watching English Change* (1994).

Peter Trudgill is Professor of English Linguistics at the University of Fribourg, Switzerland. He has also taught at the universities of Reading, Essex and Lausanne. He is the author of a number of books on dialect, and on language and society, including *Sociolinguistics* (1974; fourth edition, Penguin 2000).

D0051511

Language Myths

EDITED BY
Laurie Bauer and Peter Trudgill

PENGUIN BOOKS

PENGUIN BOOKS

Published by the Penguin Group
Penguin Books Ltd, 80 Strand, London WC2R 0RL, England
Penguin Putnam Inc., 375 Hudson Street, New York, New York 10014, USA
Penguin Books Australia Ltd, 250 Camberwell Road, Camberwell, Victoria 3124, Australia
Penguin Books Canada Ltd, 10 Alcorn Avenue, Toronto, Ontario, Canada M4V 3B2
Penguin Books India (P) Ltd, 11 Community Centre, Panchsheel Park, New Delhi – 110 017, India
Penguin Books (NZ) Ltd, Cnr Rosedale and Airborne Roads, Albany, Auckland, New Zealand
Penguin Books (South Africa) (Pty) Ltd, 24 Sturdee Avenue, Rosebank 2196, South Africa

Penguin Books Ltd, Registered Offices: 80 Strand, London WC2R 0RL, England

www.penguin.com

Published in Penguin Books 1998
23

Copyright © Laurie Bauer and Peter Trudgill, 1998
All rights reserved

The moral right of the authors has been asserted

Set in 10/12.5 pt PostScript Adobe Minion
Typeset by Rowland Phototypesetting Ltd, Bury St Edmunds, Suffolk
Printed in England by Clays Ltd, St Ives plc

Except in the United States of America, this book is sold subject
to the condition that it shall not, by way of trade or otherwise, be lent,
re-sold, hired out, or otherwise circulated without the publisher's
prior consent in any form of binding or cover other than that in
which it is published and without a similar condition including this
condition being imposed on the subsequent purchaser

ISBN-13: 978–0–140–26023–6

www.greenpenguin.co.uk

Mixed Sources
Product group from well-managed
forests and other controlled sources
www.fsc.org Cert no. SA-COC-1592
© 1996 Forest Stewardship Council

Penguin Books is committed to a sustainable future
for our business, our readers and our planet.
The book in your hands is made from paper
certified by the Forest Stewardship Council.

Contents

Contents

A Note on the Contributors

Jean Aitchison is the Rupert Murdoch Professor of Language and Communication at the University of Oxford. In her research, she is concerned with the mental lexicon, language change and the language of the media. She is the author of several books, including *Language Change: Progress or decay?* (Cambridge: Cambridge University Press, 2nd edn 1991), *Words in the Mind: An introduction to the mental lexicon* (Oxford: Blackwell, 2nd edn 1994), *The Language Web: The power and problem of words* (Cambridge: Cambridge University Press, 1997).

John Algeo is Professor Emeritus of English at the University of Georgia. He is co-author of *Origins and Development of the English Language* (Fort Worth: Harcourt Brace Jovanovich, 4th edn 1993) and author of *Fifty Years among the New Words* (Cambridge: Cambridge University Press, 1991). Editor of volume 6 of the *Cambridge History of the English Language* on English in North America, he is past President of the American Dialect Society and of the Dictionary Society of North America. For ten years he was editor of *American Speech*, the journal of the American Dialect Society, and for ten years with his wife Adele wrote the quarterly column 'Among the New Words' for that same journal.

Lars-Gunnar Andersson, Professor of Modern Swedish at the University of Gothenburg in Sweden, received his Ph.D. in linguistics in 1975 from the University of Gothenburg, where he also conducted his undergraduate studies. He has lectured at several universities and attended conferences in Europe, the USA and southern Africa. He has done most of his linguistic work in syntax, semantics, typology and sociolinguistics. He has co-written two books on the local dialect of Gothenburg and is also co-author, with two others, of *Logic in Linguistics* (Cambridge: Cambridge University Press, 1977). Together with Peter Trudgill he has written *Bad Language* (Harmondsworth: Penguin, 1990), and together with Tore Janson, *Languages in Botswana* (Gaborone: Longman Botswana, 1997). He is also a columnist on a daily newspaper in Gothenburg.

Laurie Bauer is Reader in Linguistics at Victoria University of Wellington, New Zealand. A graduate of the University of Edinburgh, he is the author of many books and articles on word-formation, international varieties of English and, most recently, language change in current English. His books include *English Word-Formation* (Cambridge: Cambridge University Press, 1983), *Introducing Linguistic Morphology* (Edinburgh: Edinburgh University Press, 1988) and *Watching English Change* (London and New York: Longman, 1994).

Winifred Bauer is a New Zealander who for over twenty years has devoted her research to the Maori language, and she has a number of publications in that field, including *Maori* (London and New York: Routledge, 1993) and the *Reed Reference Grammar of Maori* (Auckland: Reed, 1997). She has taught at Victoria University of Wellington, New Zealand, the University of Newcastle-upon-Tyne in England and Odense University in Denmark. She is an Honorary Research Fellow at Victoria University of Wellington, New Zealand.

Edward Carney read English at University College, London. He spent most of the 1950s in Sweden, teaching in the Department of English at the University of Lund. In the early 1960s he joined the newly established Department of Linguistics in the University of Manchester, where he eventually became Senior Lecturer in Phonetics. At present he is a Senior Research Fellow in the department. He is an Honorary Fellow of the Royal College of Speech and Language Therapists.

J. K. Chambers is Professor in the Department of Linguistics at the University of Toronto. As a child, he braved the howling winds on the tundra to reach the warmth of the pot-bellied stove and teacher in the one-room schoolhouse in Stoney Creek. He has written extensively about Canadian English, beginning with 'Canadian Raising' in 1973 and including *Canadian English: Origins and structures* (Toronto: Methuen, 1975), the first book on the topic. More general research includes studies of dialect acquisition, dialect topography and linguistic variation. He is co-author (with Peter Trudgill) of *Dialectology* (Cambridge: Cambridge University Press, 2nd edn 1997) and author of *Sociolinguistic Theory: Language variation and its social significance* (Oxford and New York: Blackwell, 1995).

Jenny Cheshire is Professor of Linguistics at Queen Mary and Westfield College, University of London. She has researched and published on language variation and change, modern English syntax, and different aspects of language in society. Recent editions include *English around the World: Sociolinguistic perspectives* (Cambridge: Cambridge University Press, 1991) and, with Dieter Stein, *Taming the Vernacular: From dialect to written standard language* (London and New York: Longman, 1997). She is currently writing a book on the syntax of spoken English and co-directing, with Paul Kerswill, a research project on dialect levelling in three English cities.

John H. Esling is Associate Professor of Linguistics at the University of Victoria in British Columbia, Canada. He is Secretary of the International Phonetic Association (http://www.arts.gla.ac.uk/IPA/ipa.html), and his research is on the auditory categorization of voice quality and on the phonetic production of laryngeal and pharyngeal speech sounds. He is the author of the University of Victoria Phonetic Database on CD-ROM and has participated in the development of several phonetics teaching and speech analysis software programs.

Nicholas Evans is Reader in Linguistics in the Department of Linguistics and Applied Linguistics at the University of Melbourne. Since 1980 he has worked extensively on a range of Aboriginal languages spoken in Queensland and the Northern Territory, publishing numerous articles, a grammar and dictionary of Kayardild and (with Patrick

McConvell) editing a book on linguistics and prehistory in Australia. At present he is writing a grammar of Mayali and a book on polysemy (multiple meaning) and meaning change in Australian languages.

Howard Giles (Ph.D., D.Sc., University of Bristol) is Professor and Chair of Communication at the University of California, Santa Barbara, where he also holds affiliated professorial positions in psychology and in linguistics. He is founding editor of both the *Journal of Language and Social Psychology* and the *Journal of Asian Pacific Communication*. Currently, he is President-Elect of the International Communication Association and International Association for Language and Social Psychology. His interdisciplinary research interests span the following areas of language and intergroup communication: language attitudes, ethnolinguistics, speech accommodation, intergenerational communication across cultures and police – citizen interactions.

Ray Harlow trained initially as a classicist in New Zealand and Switzerland, turning to Polynesian linguistics some twenty years ago. He is now Associate Professor in Linguistics at the University of Waikato, Hamilton, New Zealand. From its establishment by parliament in 1987 until 1993, he was a member of Te Taura Whiri i te Reo Māori (The Maori Language Commission). Recent publications and writings that relate to the topic of his contribution to this volume include: 'Lexical expansion in Maori' in *Journal of the Polynesian Society*, 102.1 (1993), pp. 99 – 107; 'A science and maths terminology for Maori' in *SAMEpapers* (Hamilton, New Zealand: University of Waikato, 1993, pp. 124 – 37); and a commissioned report to the Maori Language Commission on a comparison of the status of Maori in New Zealand and Romansh in Switzerland (1994).

Janet Holmes holds a personal Chair in Linguistics at Victoria University of Wellington, where she teaches linguistics and sociolinguistics courses. Her publications include a textbook, *An Introduction to Sociolinguistics* (London and New York: Longman, 1992) and the first book of sociolinguistic and pragmatic articles on New Zealand English, *New Zealand Ways of Speaking English* (Clevedon and Philadelphia:

Multilingual Matters, 1990), co-edited with Allan Bell. She has published on a range of topics, including New Zealand English, language and gender, sexist language, pragmatic particles and hedges, compliments and apologies. Her most recent book is *Women, Men and Politeness* (London and New York: Longman, 1995).

Anthony Lodge was formerly Professor of French at the University of Newcastle-upon-Tyne and is now Professor of French Language and Linguistics at the University of St Andrews. He has a strong interest in French language-teaching, but his work has focused primarily on the history of the French language, culminating in *French: From dialect to standard* (London and New York: Routledge, 1993), a general overview of the relationship between language and society in France since Roman times. He has recently co-authored a general introduction to the linguistic analysis of French in *Exploring the French Language* (London: Arnold, 1997). He is joint editor of the *Journal of French Language Studies* (published by Cambridge University Press).

James Milroy is Emeritus Professor of Linguistics at the University of Sheffield and now teaches at the University of Michigan. His publications include *The Language of Gerard Manley Hopkins* (London: André Deutsch, 1977), *Regional Accents of English: Belfast* (Belfast: Blackstaff, 1981), *Linguistic Variation and Change* (Oxford and Cambridge, MA: Blackwell, 1992) and, with Lesley Milroy, *Authority in Language* (London: Routledge, 1985, 2nd edn 1991). He has also written a large number of papers on sociolinguistics, historical linguistics, Middle English and Old Norse. He has recently been involved in collaborative work based in Newcastle on phonological variation and change in present-day English and is preparing a manuscript for Longman on social dialectology and language change.

Lesley Milroy has published on a wide range of topics within the general field of linguistics, including socially significant patterns of variation and change in urban dialects, processes of language standardization, bilingualism and the conversational abilities of aphasic speakers. Since 1994 she has held a professorship in linguistics at the

A Note on the Contributors

University of Michigan. She lived and worked in Belfast between 1968 and 1982, and after a year as a research fellow at the university, she moved to the University of Newcastle-upon-Tyne where she remained till 1994. She has investigated the urban dialects of both Newcastle and Belfast and has published several books and a large number of articles on these academic interests.

Michael Montgomery is Professor of English and Linguistics at the University of South Carolina, where he specializes in the history of American English and in dialects of the American South. He is editing a dictionary of Appalachian English and is writing a book on linguistic connections between Scotland and Ireland and the American South.

Nancy Niedzielski obtained her Ph.D. in linguistics from the University of California, Santa Barbara. She is an avowed interdisciplinarian working and published across areas involving creole languages and identity, sociophonetics, speech accommodation and language variation. Currently, she is co-authoring a volume with Dennis Preston on folk linguistics and working in the private sector.

Dennis R. Preston is Professor of Linguistics at Michigan State University in East Lansing. He is an old dialectologist who has been transformed into a sociolinguist. He is interested in the perception of language and language varieties by non-linguists and in attitudes towards varieties which are prejudiced against. Most recently he has been caught up in studying the facts of and attitudes towards massive ongoing vowel rotations in United States English. In addition, he has been intrigued by the parallels between sociolinguistic variation and the learning of second languages, suspecting that they may inform one another in ways not yet fully understood. Like any academic he teaches, publishes books and papers and hangs around with his cronies at conferences where he presents research findings from time to time.

Peter Roach graduated from Oxford University in psychology and philosophy and did postgraduate courses in TEFL (Manchester) and phonetics (UCL) before completing his Ph.D. at Reading University.

He was Lecturer in Phonetics at Reading University from 1968 to 1978, then moved to the University of Leeds, where he was Senior Lecturer in Phonetics from 1978 to 1991. After moving to the Department of Psychology there in 1991, he was made Professor of Cognitive Psychology. He moved back to Reading in 1994 to become Professor of Phonetics and Director of the Speech Research Laboratory; he is currently Head of the Department of Linguistic Science there. He has held many research grants for work in speech science, has published many research papers based on this work and is also author of *English Phonetics and Phonology* (Cambridge: Cambridge University Press, 2nd edn 1991) and *Introducing Phonetics* (London: Penguin, 1992). He was the principal editor of the fifteenth edition of the Daniel Jones *English Pronouncing Dictionary* (Cambridge: Cambridge University Press, 1997). He is Vice-president of the International Phonetic Association.

Peter Trudgill is Professor of English Language and Linguistics at the University of Lausanne. He was born in Norwich, England, and taught at the universities of Reading and Essex before moving to Switzerland. He is the author of three other Penguin books, *Sociolinguistics: An introduction to language and society* (1974), *Introducing Language and Society* (1992), and *Bad Language* (1990, with Lars Andersson). His other publications include *Accent, Dialect and the School* (London: Edward Arnold, 1975), *The Dialects of England* (Oxford and Cambridge, MA: Blackwell, 1990), *Dialects* (London and New York: Routledge, 1994) and *Dialects in Contact* (Oxford and New York: Blackwell, 1986).

Walt Wolfram has pioneered research on a broad range of vernacular dialects in the United States over the past three decades, including African-American Vernacular English, Appalachian English, Puerto Rican English, Native American English, and Outer Banks English. His research on African-American English in the 1960s helped launch a national awareness of the role of vernacular dialects in education and society. In 1992, after twenty-five years as Director of Research at the Center for Applied Linguistics in Washington, DC, he became the first William C. Friday Distinguished Professor at North Carolina

State, where he directs the North Carolina Language and Life Project. Recent books (with Natalie Schilling-Estes) include *Hoi Toide on the Outer Banks: The story of the Ocracoke brogue* (Chapel Hill: UNC Press, 1997) and *American English: Dialects and variation* (Oxford and New York: Blackwell, 1998).

Introduction

Laurie Bauer and Peter Trudgill

The main reason for presenting this book is that we believe that, on the whole, linguists have not been good about informing the general public about language. To see this, you have only to look at some of the major books about language aimed at a non-specialist audience which have appeared in recent years. Robert McCrum, William Cran and Robert MacNeil's *The Story of English* (New York: Viking, 1986), which derived from the TV programme of the same name, is written by an editor, a producer of current affairs films and a TV reporter. Bill Bryson's entertaining *The Mother Tongue* (London: Penguin, 1990) is written by a journalist, and Steven Pinker's *tour de force The Language Instinct* (London: Penguin, 1994) is written by a psychologist. Only David Crystal's *The Cambridge Encyclopedia of Language* (Cambridge: Cambridge University Press, 1987) and *The Cambridge Encyclopedia of the English Language* (Cambridge: Cambridge University Press, 1995) are written by a linguist. So what have the linguists been doing? And why is it that if you look at something written by the most influential linguists (Noam Chomsky, Claude Hagège, William Labov and others) you will not necessarily come away any wiser than you were when you began? The answer is that our knowledge about language has been expanding at a phenomenal rate during the latter half of the twentieth century. Linguists have been busy keeping up with that developing knowledge and explaining their own findings to other linguists. The most influential linguists are the ones who have had the most important messages for other linguists rather than for the general public. For various reasons (including the highly technical nature of some of the work), very few of them have tried to explain their findings to a lay audience. That being the case, you might wonder whether journalists, editors, poets and psychologists are not, despite everything, precisely the people who should be telling us about language. They are the ones who have had to break into the charmed circle and extract relevant information for their own needs.

Perhaps not surprisingly, we take a different line. We believe that if you want to know about human respiratory physiology you should ask a medic or a physiologist, not an athlete who has been breathing successfully for a number of years. If you want to know how an underground train works you should ask an engineer and not a commuter. And if you want to know how language works you should ask a linguist and not someone who has used language successfully in the past. In all of these cases, the reasoning is the same: users do not need to have a conscious knowledge of how a system works in order to exploit it. Explanations of the system require the type of knowledge that only the specialist can provide.

We have therefore invited some specialists – linguists – to address a number of important issues connected with language, and in this book you will find their responses. We have, though, been very specific in what we have asked them to write about, and that specificity requires some explanation. As linguists, we are very much aware that ordinary people have some well-established ideas about language. We meet these ideas when non-linguists talk to us at parties, in the common rooms of universities, from members of our families and in the media. Some of these ideas are so well established that we might say they were part of our culture. It is in this sense that we refer to them as myths (although our colleagues in mythological studies might not approve of this use of the term). But in very many cases, our reactions, as professionals, to these attitudes, to these myths, is: 'Well, it's not actually as simple as that.' Sometimes we think that the established myth is downright wrong. Sometimes we think that two things are being confused. Sometimes we think that the implications of the myth have not been thought through, or that the myth is based on a false premise, or that the myth fails to take into account some important pieces of information.

So what we have done in this book is to choose some of these pieces of cultural wisdom about language and ask professional linguists to explain why things may not be as straightforward as they seem. In each case we have tried to present as a title a brief formulation of the myth, and then we have asked the linguists to consider the idea from their professional point of view. If they think the idea is wrong, they have said so. If they think it is based on a false premise, they have said so. If they think that people may not realize where the idea comes from, they have explained this. But in every case, you will find that the linguists are not totally happy with the myth encapsulated in the title, even though they may agree with some aspects of it.

You will notice that a number of common themes appear and reappear in the chapters that follow. We consider this repetition to be a sign that, however surprising our points of view may be to non-linguists, the professional linguistics community is agreed about many fundamental issues. Some of these topics reappear because of the nature of the questions we have asked: for example, the strength of the influence of Latin upon English; the ongoing and inevitable nature of language change; the fact that different languages do similar tasks in rather different ways. You will find other such recurrent themes as you read the book. One of the recurrent themes – one that has encouraged us to produce this book – is that people in general are very concerned about the state of English and wish to know more about language.

Crucially for this book, some of the recurrent themes show the ways in which the beliefs of linguists about language may differ from the beliefs about language held in the wider community. We are agreed that all languages and dialects are complex and structured means of expression and perception, and that prejudices based on the way other people speak are akin to racism and sexism. We are agreed that most views about the superiority of one language or dialect over another have social and historical rather than genuinely linguistic origins. And we are agreed that languages and dialects are unique and miraculous products of the human brain and human society. They should be discussed respectfully and knowledgeably and, for all that we may marvel at them as objects of enormous complexity and as vehicles, sometimes, of sublime expression, they should also be discussed dispassionately and objectively if we are to achieve a better understanding of this uniquely human characteristic.

The Meanings of Words Should Not be Allowed to Vary or Change

Peter Trudgill

All languages change all the time. It is not very well understood why this is the case, but it is a universal characteristic of human languages. The only languages which do not change are those, like Latin, which nobody speaks. Languages change their pronunciations through time. Five hundred years ago, all English speakers used to pronounce the *k* in *knee* – now nobody does. Grammatical structures also change. English speakers used to say *Saw you my son?* Now everybody says *Did you see my son?* But perhaps the most obvious way in which languages change is in the usage and meaning of words.

A number of people seem to think that the fact that languages change the meanings of their words in this way is unfortunate. They believe that change in language is inherently undesirable and that we should do everything we can to stop it because change can be dangerous and confusing. In particular, any tendency for words to start to mean something which they have not always meant should be resisted.

This leads such people to argue that it makes sense to determine what a word means by looking at its origins – the *real* meaning of a word. So, for example, they would claim that it is wrong to use *aggravate* to mean 'irritate', even though this is its most common use in English, because it comes originally from Latin *aggravare*, which meant 'to make heavier' and was originally borrowed into English with the meaning 'to make more serious'. They also would maintain that it is wrong to talk about having *three alternatives*, because *alternative* comes from the Latin word *alter*, which meant 'second', and that *nice* really means 'precise' – and so on.

Actually, the history of the word *nice* provides a very good illustration of the untenable nature of this way of thinking. *Nice* comes originally from two ancient Indo-European roots, *skei* meaning 'cut', which came down into Latin as the verb *scire* 'to know', probably via a meaning such as 'be able to distinguish one thing from another', and *ne* meaning 'not'. The combination of the two forms gave the Latin verb *nescire* which meant 'to be ignorant of'. This led to the development of the adjective *nescius* 'ignorant', which came down into Old French as *nice* meaning 'silly'. It was then borrowed from French into medieval English with the meaning 'foolish, shy' and, over the centuries, has gradually changed its meaning to 'modest', then 'delicate', 'considerate', 'pleasant' and finally 'agreeable' – a very long way in 6,000 years from its original meaning. No one in their right mind, though, would argue that the 'real' meaning of *nice* is, or ought to be, 'not cutting'.

The English language is full of words which have changed their meanings slightly or even dramatically over the centuries. Changes of meaning can be of a number of different types. Some words, such as *nice*, have changed gradually. Emotive words tend to change more rapidly by losing some of their force, so that *awful*, which originally meant 'inspiring awe', now means 'very bad' or, in expressions such as *awfully good*, simply something like 'very'. In any case, all connection with 'awe' has been lost.

Some changes of meaning, though, seem to attract more attention than others. This is perhaps particularly the case where the people who worry about such things believe that a distinction is being lost. For example, there is a lot of concern at the moment about the words *uninterested* and *disinterested*. In modern English, the positive form *interested* has two different meanings. The first and older meaning is approximately 'having a personal involvement in', as in

He is an interested party in the dispute.

The second and later, but now much more common, meaning is 'demonstrating or experiencing curiosity in, enthusiasm for, concern for', as in

He is very interested in cricket.

It is not a problem that this word has more than one meaning. Confusion never seems to occur, largely because the context will normally make it obvious which meaning is intended. In all human languages there are very many words which have more than one meaning – this is a very common and entirely normal state of affairs. Most English speakers, for example, can instantly think of a number of different meanings for the words *common* and *state* and *affairs* which I have just used.

Perhaps surprisingly, according to dictionaries the two different meanings of *interested* have different negative forms. The negative of the first meaning is *disinterested*, as in

He is an interested party in the dispute, and I am disinterested and therefore able to be more objective about it.

Disinterested is thus roughly equivalent to 'neutral, impartial'. The negative form of the second, more usual meaning is *uninterested*, as in

He is very interested in cricket, but I am uninterested in all sports.

Uninterested is thus roughly equivalent to 'bored, feeling no curiosity'.

Now it happens that *interested*, in its original meaning, is today a rather unusual, learned, formal word in English. Most people, if they wanted to convey this concept in normal everyday speech, would probably say something like *not neutral*, or *biased* or *involved* or *concerned*. Recently, this unfamiliarity with the older meaning of the word *interested* has led to many people now using *disinterested* with the same meaning as *uninterested*:

I'm disinterested in cricket.

They have, perhaps, heard the word *disinterested* and, not being aware of the meaning 'neutral, unbiased', they have started using it as the negative form of *interested* in the more recent sense. Opponents of this change claim that this is an ignorant misuse of the word, and that a very useful distinction is being lost. What can we say about this?

We can notice that this relatively sudden change of meaning is rather different from the changes of meaning we discussed above in the case of *awful* and *nice*, which seem to have changed gradually over long periods of time. But, all the same, it is not something which is particularly surprising to students of language change. The English prefix *dis-* is very commonly employed to turn positive adjectives into negative adjectives. In this way, *pleasing, honest, fluent, agreeable* become *displeasing, dishonest, disfluent, disagreeable*. (Note also that *displeasing* and *unpleasing* both occur with approximately identical meanings, although *displeasing* is more common.) We cannot therefore be surprised if, by analogy, speakers start following this pattern of using *dis-* to make a negative form out of the newer meaning of *interested*.

We also have to point out to opponents of this change that there are actually some benefits to be gained from this development. For example, there now seems to be a tendency for speakers to make a small difference of meaning between the two forms. This is something which very often happens to synonyms – they very rarely stay complete synonyms. So *disinterested* often seems to be stronger in meaning than *uninterested*, with the former indicating real, positive lack of interest, perhaps even hostility, while *uninterested* refers to simple apathy or indifference.

Even more useful is the fact that we now have something which we never had before – the possibility of a single-word noun corresponding to the adjective. There was never a word *uninterestedness* or *uninterest* in English, so we had to use rather clumsy, longer noun-phrases such as *lack of interest*, which I just used above. Now, however, we can say things like

John demonstrated considerable disinterest in the game of cricket.

But are there also any difficulties caused by this change? Are those who resist the change right to do so? Surely confusion can result from this development? Actually, it does not seem so. For many people, of course, there was never any danger of confusion because they did not know or did not use *disinterested* in its original meaning anyway. But even for those perhaps more educated people who did and do make a distinction, there do not seem to be any problems of comprehension.

As usually happens with words with more than one meaning, the context in which the word is used nearly always makes it clear which meaning is intended. After all, we never seem to get confused about the two different meanings of *interested*, so why should we be confused if *disinterested* has two meanings also? We will not usually confuse the meaning of *common* in 'Chaffinches are very common in England' with its meaning in 'Only common people eat peas with their knife'. We are very unlikely to misinterpret the meaning of *state* on hearing 'Slovakia has become an independent state' as opposed to 'John was in a very bad state'. How many people would confuse the meaning of *affairs* in 'Mary's husband left her because she kept having affairs with other men' with its meaning in 'Mary is very busy at her office and has many different affairs to attend to'? Equally,

The school children looked very disinterested

is not likely to be ambiguous, and nor is

As an arbitrator, they need someone who is completely disinterested.

This is true of a number of other pairs of words which dictionaries distinguish between, but for which many speakers and writers make no difference. One such well-known pair is *imply* and *infer*. Dictionaries, and schoolteachers, tell us that these two words mean different things, and that they should be used differently. So,

She implied that he was stupid

means that, by something she said, she hinted or gave clues to the effect that he was stupid, without actually saying so outright. On the other hand,

She inferred that he was stupid

means that his behaviour or speech was such that she was able to deduce from it that he was stupid. However, many people in the English-speaking world who do not read dictionaries or do not listen to what their schoolteachers tell them are liable to use *infer* with the meaning that the dictionary says should be confined to *imply*:

Are you inferring I'm stupid?

Now, it is undoubtedly true that if you use *infer* in this way, there are people around who will infer that you are uneducated or careless. But it is very unlikely indeed that there will be any actual confusion of meaning. Even if the situational context does not make it clear what is meant, the grammatical context will: if I imply something *to* you, you will, if you are clever and sensitive enough, infer that same something *from* what I have said. This is a distinction which can just as well be made, then, by means of *infer to* and *infer from*.

The same can be said of certain other pairs of words which are related to each other in this way. The technical term for such pairs is *converse terms*. Examples are *lend* and *borrow*, and *learn* and *teach*. They are converse terms because, if you lend me something, I necessarily borrow it from you. *Lend* and *learn* vary in usage between one dialect of English and another. In some dialects, including Standard English, they are always distinguished. Many English speakers of other dialects, however, do not observe the distinctions enshrined in dictionaries, and say things like

Can I lend your bike?

and

The teacher learnt us geography.

Purists might want to argue that we should not permit potentially confusing variation of this type between dialects. But, once again, it is clear that absolutely no confusion of meaning can result, and that speakers of the different dialects will always understand one another even if they follow different patterns of usage. The context, and/or the use of prepositions like *from* and *to*, will make it clear what is intended. It is therefore difficult to argue that there is anything particularly reprehensible in failing to observe such distinctions. (Actually, it is not only dialects of English which vary in this way. Individual languages differ from one another quite a lot in the extent to which they use different words for converse terms. The German verb *leihen*, for example, means both 'to lend' and 'to borrow', something which causes German speakers no distress whatsoever.)

But – to go back to *disinterested* – what should we say about the claims of 'ignorance' and 'misuse'? It is certainly true that those people who originally started saying *disinterested* in the new way probably did not know its other meaning. We could then say that they were misusing the word. There is a very important observation we can make about this, though. The fact is that none of us can unilaterally decide what a word means. Meanings of words are shared between people – they are a kind of social contract we all agree to – otherwise communication would not be possible. If somebody decides all by themselves that *nice* ought to mean 'ignorant' because that is what it meant originally in English, he or she will have a very hard time. If I said 'Because they do not study very hard, my students are very nice,' it is certain that people would misunderstand me and probable that they would think that I was mad. Similarly, it is certain that anyone who found Salisbury cathedral enormously impressive and said 'I find this building really awful' would also be completely misunderstood.

The same is likely to be the case in future with *disinterested*. If we ask the question 'When is misuse not misuse?', the answer is clearly 'When everybody does it'. If, in 200 years' time, all English speakers use *disinterested* in the new way, which they probably will, the language will perhaps have lost something, but it will also have gained something, as we have seen above – and we will no longer be able to talk of misuse, even though the initial change may have occurred because of lack of knowledge of the original meaning.

In any case, it is clear that even if the worriers regard this change as undesirable, there is nothing they can do about it. Words do not mean what we as individuals might wish them to mean, but what speakers of the language in general want them to mean. These meanings can and do change as they are modified and negotiated in millions of everyday exchanges over the years between one speaker and another. Language change cannot be halted. Nor should the worriers feel obliged to try to halt it. Languages are self-regulating systems which can be left to take care of themselves. They are self-regulating because their speakers want to understand each other and be understood. If there is any danger of misunderstanding, speakers and writers will appreciate this possibility and guard against it by avoiding synonyms, or by giving extra context, as in the well-known

I mean funny ha-ha, not funny peculiar.

There is nothing at all funny-peculiar about the fact that some words in modern English are currently changing their meanings.

I would like to thank Malgorzata Fabiszak, Jean Hannah and Ian Kirby for their comments and advice on earlier versions of this chapter.

Source

Lars Andersson and Peter Trudgill, *Bad Language* (Oxford: Blackwell, 1990; and London: Penguin, 1990).

MYTH 2

Some Languages are Just Not Good Enough

Ray Harlow

If we look at the languages spoken in the world today, we notice very wide differences in the use to which they are put. Most languages are the first language of some community and serve the everyday functions of that community perfectly well. A few languages have a more restricted range of uses, for instance, until recently, Latin was restricted to certain uses within the Roman Catholic Church, particularly the conduct of services and formal communication internationally within the Church. Now its use is even more restricted and it is really only now used by a few people to read the literature originally written in that language.

On the other hand, some languages have wider functions than that of everyday communication and are used as official languages in the administration of whole states and nations, in education to the highest levels and in literature of all kinds. Yet other languages enjoy an international role, English perhaps being the best example of this at the moment. English is the language of international air traffic, business communication, scientific publication and the lingua franca of tourism. Unfortunately, the differences in the range of roles that languages play frequently lead some people to believe that some languages which do not fulfil a wide range of functions are in fact incapable of doing so. In the view of some people, some languages are just not good enough. Not only do they not act as languages of science, of international communication, of high literature, they are inherently inferior and could not be used in these ways.

This sort of opinion can be seen particularly strikingly in societies where a minority language is spoken alongside a major language. A case of this kind is the situation of Maori, the indigenous Polynesian

9

language of New Zealand. Linguists estimate that English is the first language of some 95 per cent of the New Zealand population and the only language of about 90 per cent. People who identify themselves as Maori make up about 12 per cent of the New Zealand population of just over 3 million, but although the Maori language is regarded as a very important part of identity as a Maori, it is spoken fluently by perhaps 30,000 people. Because of social changes in New Zealand within the past five decades or so, Maori has seen its uses increasingly restricted till in many places it is now only used at formal institutionalized events.

Over the last twenty years or so, there have been a number of initiatives in the areas of politics, education and broadcasting to try to reverse the trend and, as a result, Maori is now an official language of New Zealand, is used in radio and television broadcasting and is not only a subject of study but also the language in which teaching is carried out at a number of schools and even at one university.

As these initiatives have progressed, it has been possible to notice in the reaction of some people the very attitude I have been referring to, that Maori is simply not capable of being used as an official language or as the language of education beyond the very basic level. Sometimes, the expression of this opinion reveals that it is in fact not based on logic. I recall a comment in a New Zealand newspaper some years ago, which tried to make the point that Maori was no good as a language because it had to borrow words from English in order to express new ideas. English on the other hand could be seen to be a very flexible and vital language because it had throughout its history been able to draw resources from all over the place to express new ideas!

However, it is not only in this sort of situation that we can encounter the idea that some languages are just not up to it. Cicero, the Roman orator, politician and philosopher of the first century BC, composed his philosophical works in Latin partly to make Greek philosophy available to a Latin-speaking audience, but also partly to show that it could be done. This was because some of his contemporaries were sceptical about the possibility of Latin being able to express the ideas and trains of thought of the Greeks! In their view, Latin was just not good enough. However, this was a language which went on to be the language of scholarship, science, international diplomacy and literature for well over a millennium! Sir Isaac Newton, the famous scholar of the seventeenth century, published his ideas in Latin.

The same sort of thing occurred again in Western Europe at the end of the Middle Ages, as the so-called vernacular languages took over functions that had previously been the domain of Latin. At this time, there were people who believed that the emerging languages like French, English, Italian, and so on were too unpolished, immature and lacking in resources to be able to convey the abstract thought and breadth of knowledge usually expressed in the ancient languages of Latin and Greek.

Why are some languages not good enough?

Let's look briefly at the ways in which languages are supposed to be inadequate, in what respects they are not good enough and also at the question: 'Not good enough for what?'

In some instances, it is features of the structure of a language which are picked on as the reason why another language is to be preferred for a particular function. In the south-east of Switzerland, many people still speak a language descended from the Latin of the Roman colonists. It is called Romansh and is still the everyday language in a number of villages and regions, though German has been making inroads in the area for centuries. As with Maori, which I mentioned above, there has been a push in recent decades to increase the areas of life and activity in which Romansh is used. Now, German is a language which can very easily combine words into what are called 'compounds'. Romansh is a language which cannot do this so readily and instead uses phrases as a way of combining ideas. Some speakers of Romansh have reacted to this structural difference by believing that Romansh is not good enough to be used in really technical areas of life because 'German is able to construct clearly defined single words for technical ideas, Romansh is not.' This notion ignores the facts that other languages such as French and Italian are in exactly the same boat as Romansh yet obviously have no problem in being precise in technical areas, and that Romansh had for centuries been the language in which all the aspects, some of them very 'technical', of an alpine agricultural society were dealt with.

This kind of view is not unlike the 'myth' discussed in Myth 10: Some Languages Have No Grammar, the myth that because languages differ in the way they work structurally, they also differ in the extent to which they can express logical connections between words and ideas. In other instances, the reason why a language is 'just not good enough' is that 'it is ugly, rude, barbaric.' This is one of the reasons why some people felt that the vernacular languages were incapable of assuming the roles that Latin played. As one scholar has put it, the common languages were redolent of 'the stench of dung and the sweat of the warrior'.

Even Dante, who was a champion for the cause of the use of vernaculars and is credited with the establishment of modern Italian, in his survey of Italian dialects in search of a suitable one for his literary purposes, ruled out the Roman dialect because 'of all Italian vernaculars, their wretched savage noise is the most foul – and no wonder, since it matches the depravity and coarseness of their ways.'

These two examples in fact point to what is really going on here. This is a matter which is taken up more fully in Myth 11: Italian is Beautiful, German is Ugly. It turns out that people will often transfer to a language or dialect their opinions of the people whose language or dialect it is. Thus, Dante saw the Roman dialect as savage and wretched because this was his opinion of the Roman people of his time.

The third reason given for the view that a language is not good enough is rather more serious; it is the argument that 'X is not good enough because you can't discuss nuclear physics in it.' The implication is that English (or some other language like German or Russian, for instance) is a better language than X because there are topics you can discuss in one but not the other. At first glance this seems a very telling argument. There are things you can do in one language but not another, therefore some languages are better than others, therefore some languages are not good enough at least for some purposes.

However, this view confuses a feature of languages which is due just to their history with an inherent property of languages. That is, this opinion concludes that because there has been no occasion or need to discuss, for argument's sake, nuclear physics in Maori, it could never be done because of some inherent fault in Maori. A little thought, however, will show that this argument cannot be maintained. Computers were not discussed in Old English; Modern English is the same language as Old English, only later; it should follow that Modern English cannot be used to discuss computers. This is clearly absurd. What of course has happened is that through time English has developed the resources necessary to the discussion of computers and very many other topics which were simply unknown in earlier times. In order for us to discuss some topic in a particular language, that language must provide us with words to refer to the various aspects of our topic; it must have the appropriate vocabulary. Of course the language must also provide ways of combining the words to form statements, questions, and so on. But all languages have these ways. This is a theme which will be taken up below in other chapters, especially, Myth 10: Some Languages Have No Grammar and Myth 4: French is a Logical Language. Essentially, languages may differ as to the way various aspects of structure are handled, but they are all capable of expressing the same range of structural meanings.

Not all languages have the same vocabulary though. It is true that some languages have developed vocabularies to deal with topics which are just not discussed in some other languages. And 'developed' is the crucial word in this matter. English can discuss nuclear physics because, over the centuries, as scientific thought has developed, it has acquired the vocabulary to deal with the new developments; it has not always been there as an inherent feature of English. Rather, English expanded its vocabulary in a variety of ways over the centuries so as to meet the new demands being made of it. All languages are capable of the same types of expansion of vocabulary to deal with whatever new areas of life their speakers need to talk about.

If one looks at the words which are used in English to handle technical subjects, and indeed many non-technical ones as well, one sees that in fact the vast majority of these words have actually come from some other language and been incorporated into English. This process is usually called 'borrowing', though there is no thought that the words will be given back somehow! All languages do this to some extent, though English is perhaps the language which has the highest level of 'borrowed' vocabulary, at least among the world's major languages.

However, this is by no means the only way in which a language can develop its vocabulary; there are many cases where a language's vocabulary is developed 'from within', that is, by using its own existing resources. Sometimes, but by no means always, this path is followed by a language and its speakers, if there is a notion that borrowing will hurt the language. Another reason why a language's own resources may be used in the expansion of its vocabulary is because a writer wants his/her work to be readily understood by its intended audience, who might be put off by too much borrowing. This is what Cicero did. In order to write in Latin about the ideas of Greek philosophy, he had to develop a Latin vocabulary which corresponded to the ideas he wanted to put across. Most of the time he did this by taking a particular Latin word and deliberately assigning it a technical meaning. A particularly important example of this was his use of the Latin word *ratio* to mean 'reason', a usage which has come down to us today in English. On other occasions, he invented new words made up of Latin elements, for instance, the word *qualitas*, which became of course 'quality' in English, was deliberately coined by Cicero to correspond to a Greek idea.

Minority languages, like Maori and Romansh, are today doing very much the same thing as Cicero did for Latin, constructing vocabulary out of existing resources within the languages, precisely so that they can be used to talk about areas like computers, law, science, and so on, for which they have not been used so much in the past. These two languages are unlikely ever to become international languages of science or diplomacy, but if history had been different, they could have, and then we might have been wondering whether perhaps English was 'just not good enough'.

The Media are Ruining English

Jean Aitchison

English is sick, maybe even fatally ill, judging from complaints: 'The language the world is crying out to learn is diseased in its own country,' moaned one anxious worrier. 'Oh, please, English-lovers everywhere, do your bit for the language. Let's stop this slide down the slippery slope ... before communication becomes a frustrating exercise we are unable to face,' urged another.

This morbid concern for the health of English is not new. In every decade, language 'defenders' pop up like sentries before old castles. They behave as if they alone are preventing the language from crumbling into dust. As the writer Thomas Lounsbury commented in 1908:

There seems to have been in every period of the past, as there is now, a distinct apprehension in the minds of very many worthy persons that the English tongue is always in the condition approaching collapse, and that arduous efforts must be put forth, and put forth persistently, in order to save it from destruction.

The delusion that our language is sick is therefore a recurring one. What changes are the culprits of this supposed linguistic slide? These vary. Parents, teachers, the press, have all been blamed. But in recent years, the media – television, radio, newspapers – have been widely criticized as linguistic criminals. To take a typical example:

... what I find ... hard ... to stomach these days is the pidgin being served up more and more by television and radio as well as the press ... Only Canute's courtiers would deny that language is a living thing ...

But the increasingly rapid spread of what I can only describe as Engloid throughout the all-pervasive communications media foreshadows an anarchy that must eventually defeat the whole object of communication – to understand and be understood . . .

Even in the last century, journalists were regarded as linguistic troublemakers: 'Among writers, those who do the most mischief are . . . the men generally who write for the newspapers,' commented a writer on 'popular errors in language' (1880). 'Many causes exist which tend to corrupt the "well of English undefiled" . . . [One] is the immense extension and influence of the newspaper press . . .' lamented another (1889). He continued: 'The newspaper press of the United States and the British colonies, as well as the inferior class of newspapers in this country, is to a large extent in the hands of writers who have no respect for the propriety or reticence of language.'

In the twentieth century, complaints about media language have escalated, above all because of the advent of radio and television. This has added concern about spoken speech to that about written: 'We are plagued with idiots on radio and television who speak English like the dregs of humanity,' bemoaned one letter-writer. 'I have two young children . . . who try to keep afloat in a flood of sloppy speech poured at them from the television set,' raged another.

The objections range over all aspects of language. When the 'Top Twenty' complaints about broadcast language were listed by David Crystal in 1982, he found that nine related to grammar (the way words are combined), six were about pronunciation (the way words were articulated) and five about vocabulary (the particular words used).

Disliked usages are frequently assumed by grumblers to be new, a sign of modern decadence. Yet, as Crystal commented, many have been around for a long time. Top of the 'Top Twenty' complaints was the supposed misuse of *you and I* versus *you and me*. Yet around 400 years ago, in Shakespeare's *The Merchant of Venice*, the merchant Antonio says: 'All debts are cleared *between you and I*,' so breaking the supposed 'rule' that *you and me* is the 'correct' form after a preposition. In the late-eighteenth century a writer commented on 'the phrase *between you and I*, which tho' it must be confessed to be ungrammatical, is yet almost universally used in familiar conversation.' And in the last ten years, Oxford-educated Lady Thatcher proclaimed: 'It's not for *you and I* to condemn the Malawi economy.' So this is not a 'new' phenomenon.

So if media usages which upset language worriers are often old ones, why do so many people complain about 'modern decadence' and 'journalistic incompetence'?

Two interwoven misunderstandings underlie complaints about media language. First, a 'dirty fingernails' fallacy, a notion that journalists are sloppy language users. Second, a 'garbage heap' fallacy, a false belief that 'journalism is junk writing.' Let us consider each in turn.

Dirty fingernails fallacy: journalists use language sloppily

According to the 'dirty fingernails' fallacy, journalists do not pay sufficient attention to language details: they never bother to scrub their linguistic fingernails clean, as it were. On closer inspection, this is untrue. The fallacy is largely due to ignorance about how language changes – perhaps not surprisingly, since how change happens has become clear only in the last thirty or so years.

Until around 1960 language change was regarded as a slow and mysterious process, rather like the budding and blooming of flowers – something hard to see, however long you stare. A popular view in the 1950s was that change occurred when speakers somehow missed their linguistic target and drifted away from the original norm. One word was assumed to turn into another over time, like a tadpole slowly transforming itself into a frog.

Yet this tadpole-to-frog view of change is now outdated. In recent years a 'young cuckoo' model has replaced it. This new, more realistic viewpoint arose largely from the pioneering work of the American sociolinguist William Labov. Competition rather than metamorphosis is at the root of language alterations, he demonstrated. A new variant arises in some section of the community and competes with an existing one. Then the newer form is likely to expand and gradually oust the older ones, like a young cuckoo pushing a previous occupant out of the nest. Old and new forms therefore coexist and compete: the old is not magically transformed into the new.

These young cuckoo takeovers typically have a slow beginning, then a sudden upsurge. A form first creeps in among a subsection of the population. The word *gay* for 'homosexual' had long been in use in San Francisco before it expanded its territory and pushed aside other terms such as *queer, poof*. The term *wimp* for 'feeble male' had also been around for years in California before it gradually ousted other words for 'weak or insignificant person' such as *nebbish, nerd, weed*. The older words get used less and less often and gradually dwindle away. But the media did not initiate these changes; they were reflecting current usage.

The prefix *mini-* provides a blueprint for the slow beginning and sudden upswing of a typical change. It also illustrates the role of the media. The prefix occurred as early as 1845, when the *Scotsman* newspaper carried a notice of an 'important sale of horses, harness, and carriages', which included 'one excellent 12-inside omnibus' and 'one handsome minibus', both horse-drawn. A fairly long time elapsed before sporadic other *mini-* forms arrived in the language: *mini-camera* came in the 1930s, *mini-piano* in the 1940s. The prefix therefore gradually crept into the language, like a bit-player in a drama.

Take-off point came in the 1960s when *mini-cab, mini-van* and other transport words became widely used, alongside clothing words, such as *mini-skirt* and *mini-dress*. Then *mini-* started appearing on other types of word: a *mini-boom* occurred in economics, a *mini-bar* became standard in some hotel rooms, *mini-computers* were widely used, and a writer commented that he must have been out of his *mini-mind*.

The media nurtured the *mini-* explosion by reporting the news. *Vogue*, the fashion magazine, noted *mini-skirt* first in 1965. Television produced several *mini-series*. Newspapers also joined in. A total of 125 stories contained a *mini-* prefix in *The Times* and *Sunday Times* in the first three months of 1993, for example.

The media are therefore linguistic mirrors: they reflect current language usage and extend it. Journalists are observant reporters who pick up early on new forms and spread them to a wider audience.

They do not normally invent these forms, nor are they corrupting the language.

Radio and television reproduce the various ways of speaking we hear around, they do not invent them. Often, several different ways of pronouncing the same word co-exist. This worries some people. In a recent radio talk, the speaker referred to *kilOmetres*, a pronunciation which attracted angry letters, such as:

I was astonished to hear you pronounce kIlometre *as* kilOmetre ... *Surely, even if it is argued that language has no rights or wrongs, but merely usage, there IS sense and nonsense. The pronunciation* kilOmetre *is in the latter category,* kIlometre *in the former.*

Yet both pronunciations are common, according to a survey carried out by the editor of the *Longman Pronunciation Dictionary* (1990): 52 per cent preferred the older *kIlometre* and 48 per cent the newer *kilOmetre*. This type of fluctuation suggests that a change is underway. The main pronunciation grumble in David Crystal's 'Top Twenty' complaints was about the stress on words such as *controversy*. The survey found that 44 per cent preferred *CONtroversy*, and 56 per cent *conTROVersy*, indicating that both are acceptable.

The *kilometre* and *controversy* complaints are puzzling: the altered stress is fairly trivial and does not affect understanding. Perhaps worriers are working with an outdated view of language: an old 'for want of a nail' image is embedded in some people's minds, the old proverb in which a lost nail led to a lost battle: 'For want of a nail, a shoe was lost, for want of a shoe, a horse was lost, for want of a horse a man was lost, for want of a man, a battle was lost.' Lack of care over 'linguistic fingernails' is presumed to lead to language collapse. But metaphors which apply to one area of life do not necessarily apply to others. The 'young cuckoo' image is a more realistic one. Furthermore, the young cuckoos cannot unbalance language. English, like any tongue, maintains its own patterns and keeps itself organized: a language, like a thermostat, regulates itself constantly. Some inbuilt property in the human mind maintains all languages, everywhere.

Garbage heap fallacy: journalism is junk writing

The 'garbage heap' fallacy is a false belief that 'journalism is junk writing.' Yet writing for the press is a demanding skill. The public reads newspapers avidly because they are written in a way which attracts attention and then sustains it. Such writing requires training and practice. Newcomers may flounder, as satirized by Evelyn Waugh in his novel *Scoop*. The hero, Boot, is a novice writer who pens a bi-weekly half-column on nature: 'Feather-footed through the plashy fen passes the questing vole . . .' He is mistaken for a top journalist and sent to a world trouble-spot. His heart heavy with misgiving, he types the first news report of his career:

Nothing much has happened except to the president who has been imprisoned in his own palace by revolutionary junta . . . They say he is drunk when his children try to see him but governess says most unusual. Lovely spring weather. Bubonic plague raging.

Compare this with a typical 'real' newspaper report:

Up to six people were feared dead and 60 injured yesterday after a cargo ship lost power and ploughed into a busy shopping mall built on a wharf in the American port of New Orleans.

Here the writer has specified what happened, where it happened, when it happened, who was involved, how it happened in thirty-five words – a so-called 'hard news formula'. It's clear, it's informative and, in the words of George Orwell, it uses 'language as an instrument for expressing and not for concealing or preventing thought'. Orwell, best known as the author of the novels *Animal Farm* and *Nineteen Eighty-Four*, was a successful journalist as well as a best-selling novelist. He pointed out the importance of making one's meaning clear. For doing this, he provided 'rules that one can rely on when instinct fails'. Below, slightly rephrased, are his six guidelines, which trainee journalists are still taught to follow:

1. If it's possible to cut out a word, cut it out.
2. Never use a long word where a short will do.
3. Never use a passive if you can use an active.
4. Avoid foreign and technical words.
5. Never use a metaphor you've seen in print.
6. Break these rules to avoid something outlandish.

Readers may dispute the choice of newspaper content: 'An editor is one who separates the wheat from the chaff and prints the chaff,' according to Adlai Stevenson. The blood-and-guts detail of a recent murder may disgust some, the convolutions of a film star's love-life may bore others. But the language in which the murders and marriages are recounted is likely to be lucid and polished. Journalists generally follow the advice not only of George Orwell but also of Joel Chandler Harris, the nineteenth-century author of *Uncle Remus*. Harris worked as a journalist for a large part of his life. He advised:

> *When you've got a thing to say,*
> *Say it! Don't take half a day . . .*
> *Life is short – a fleeting vapour –*
> *Don't you fill the whole blamed paper*
> *With a tale, which at a pinch,*
> *Could be covered in an inch!*
> *Boil her down until she simmers,*
> *Polish her until she glimmers.*

Samuel Johnson, the eighteenth-century dictionary-writer, once said: 'I never open up a newspaper without finding something I should have deemed it a loss not to have seen; never without deriving from it instruction and amusement.' He does not specify what kind of 'instruction' he was seeking. But almost certainly, if he looked at a newspaper today, he would learn both about the modern language and how to use it clearly.

Sources and further reading

How and why language changes is discussed in Jean Aitchison, *Language Change: Progress or decay?* (Cambridge: Cambridge University Press, 2nd edn 1991). Worries about language decline and the role of the media in change are explored in Jean Aitchison, *Language Joyriding* (Inaugural lecture at Oxford University, Oxford: Clarendon Press, 1994); Jean Aitchison, *The Language Web: The power and problem of words* (BBC 1996 Reith Lectures, Cambridge: Cambridge University Press, 1997). Attitudes to language are documented in Richard Bailey, *Images of English: A cultural history of the language* (Ann Arbor: University of Michigan Press, 1991; Cambridge: Cambridge University Press, 1992), which contains the Thomas Lounsbury quote about perpetual worriers. The 'Top Twenty' complaints about the radio were listed in David Crystal, 'Language on the air – has it degenerated?' (*Listener*, 9 July 1981, pp. 37–9).

The skill involved in writing for the media is dissected in 'How to do it' books, such as Nicholas Bagnall, *Newspaper Language* (Oxford: Focal Press, 1993) and Andrew Boyd, *Broadcast Journalism: Techniques of radio and TV news* (Oxford: Focal Press, 3rd edn 1994), who quotes the lines from Joel Chandler Harris. The novice writer Boot is in Evelyn Waugh, *Scoop* (London: Chapman and Hall, 1938; Penguin Books, 1943). Orwell's good-writing precepts are in his essay 'Politics and the English language' (1946), reprinted in George Orwell, *Inside the Whale and Other Essays* (London: Penguin, 1962).

MYTH 4

French is a Logical Language
Anthony Lodge

French people have been claiming that theirs is a logical language for
the past three and a half centuries, though what they mean when they
say this is rather obscure – which is a pity, since the other adjective
they use to describe French, along with 'logical', is the word 'clear',
as we shall see.

In 1647 the father of all French purist grammarians – Claude Favre
de Vaugelas – referred to 'clarity of language the which property
French possesses over all other languages in the world,' and he was
swiftly followed by people who asserted things like, 'we [the French]
in everything we say follow exactly the order of rational thought,
which is the order of Nature.'

The most celebrated expression of this idea came in 1784 when a
self-styled aristocrat (Count Antoine de Rivarol, 1753–1801) won the
prize for the best essay presented at the Berlin Academy that year.
Actually, 'Count' Rivarol was the son of an innkeeper in the southern
French town of Bagnols, but he knew there was little hope of advance-
ment unless such an unfortunate fact could be disguised. The title of
his prize-winning essay was: 'Concerning the universality of the French
language', and the author's aim was to explain why French was used
by all the toffs and intellectuals of Europe (including students at the
Berlin Academy) in preference to other languages, even their own.
Of course, it had nothing whatsoever to do with the fact that France
had been 'top nation' in Europe for a century and a half. French, he
believed, was preferred by all rational-minded people on account of
its inherently logical structure:

What distinguishes our language from the ancient and the modern languages is the order and structure of the sentence. This order must always be direct and necessarily clear. In French the subject of the discourse is named first, then the verb which is the action, and finally the object of this action: this is the natural logic present in all human beings . . .

French syntax is incorruptible. It is from this that results this admirable clarity which is the eternal basis of our language. What is not clear is not French: what is not clear is still English, Italian, Greek or Latin.

Given the importance Rivarol attaches in sentence three to placing the subject before the verb in order to establish the logical credentials of French, it is unfortunate that he should himself place the subject ('this admirable clarity') after the verb ('results') in sentence five. However, difficulties such as this have not stood in the way of successive generations of teachers and commentators peddling similar ideas.

In the nineteenth century C. Allou – a mining engineer turned grammarian – reproduced Rivarol's thoughts almost verbatim: 'One of the chief characteristics of French is its extreme clarity which renders it less susceptible than any other language to obscurity, ambiguity and double-meaning.' The distinguished critic F. Brunetière went one better: 'People have often vaunted the "clarity", the "logic", the "precision" of the French language, and they have been right. However, it is not the French language which is in itself clearer and more logical than the others, it is French thinking.'

Not all were agreed, however, about the ability of the inarticulate masses to do justice to the superlative qualities of their language. Many French people were felt unworthy of the treasure bestowed upon them. In 1910 Abbé C. Vincent declared, 'Our national language, so clear, so subtle, so logical, so distinguished, is becoming increasingly fuzzy, turgid, deformed and vulgar.'

However, as the Great War approached, the French closed ranks. Claims about the intellectual qualities of French and of the French usually become shriller and more chauvinistic as the French nation comes under threat from outside – from the Germans, for instance, or from the Anglo-Saxons. On the eve of the First World War J. Payot announced, 'We find everywhere among French people the courageous striving after clarity.' In the hey-day of Gaullist hostility to American influence in France, J. Duron declared in 1963:

I consider precision and clarity to be the prime qualities of our language . . . to such an extent that I doubt whether there has ever existed, since the time of the Greeks, a language which reflected thought so transparently . . .

And it is in precisely this area that the French language has for a long time had the reputation of being beyond compare. Well handled, it makes clear the most difficult ideas, and this is one of the reasons for its long domination in Europe . . .

It carries further than any other language the requirement and the capacity for clarity.

Such drum-banging in favour of the French language is not the monopoly of the conservative right. Even the socialist President Mitterrand was drawn into it:

On the subject of the French language, after so many others it is hard to add further praising words to those so often repeated concerning its rigour, its clarity, its elegance, its nuances, the richness of its tenses and its moods, the delicacy of its sounds, the logic of its word order.

It is perhaps understandable that this myth about French should have had a strong hold on the minds of native speakers of the language, but it is a little surprising that it should be shared by distinguished professors of French in Britain:

In translating English prose into French we shall often find that the meaning of the text is not clear and definite . . . Looseness of reasoning and lack of logical sequence are our common faults . . . The French genius is clear and precise . . . In translating into French we thus learn the lesson of clarity and precision. –Ritchie and Moore

It is even more surprising when we find eminent linguists pushing the idea:

The seventeenth century, which believed it could bend everything to the demands of reason, undoubtedly gave logic the opportunity to transform the French language in the direction of reason. Even today it is clear that it conforms much more closely to the demands of pure logic than any other language. – W. von Wartburg

What are people thinking of when they make claims like these about the inherent logic and clarity of the French language? The implication contained in all of the quotations we have looked at is that the structure of French is miraculously closer to that of pure, language-free thought ('mentalese', as Steven Pinker expresses it) than the structure of other languages. Indeed, we have seen how French commentators have regarded their language as the universal language to which all rational human beings naturally aspire in spite of themselves and in spite of their own mother tongue. Allegedly, French syntax follows very closely the order of logical thought processes; allegedly, the organization of French grammar and vocabulary coincides with the natural ordering of time and space; and French style allegedly clothes ideas in a simpler and more elegant garb than is to be found elsewhere. Let us look at each of these notions briefly in turn.

French syntax follows the order of logic

The argument most frequently advanced in defence of the logicality of French is that based on word order: just as 'in logic' the agent precedes the action, which precedes the patient, so the fundamental word order of French (unlike that of Latin and German) is Subject + Verb + Object. This argument is suspect on several counts. Firstly, French is by no means the only language to be of the SVO type – so is that language which Rivarol found so terribly unclear and illogical, English. Secondly, it is legitimate to ask just how fundamental the SVO order is in French. In formal style cases of inversion of Subject and Verb are quite common, as Rivarol himself unwittingly demon-strated.

O   V   S
e.g. *Sans doute vous écrira-t-elle* = No doubt she will write to you

In informal style 'dislocated structures' like the following are the rule rather than the exception.

O   S   V
e.g. *Mon chien, je l'ai perdu* = I have lost my dog

Moreover, if we base our argument on meaning rather than on grammatical function, all passive sentences in French become a breach of the so-called natural order.

patient   action   agent
e.g. *Le vieillard a été soigné par un guérisseur* = The old chap was looked after by a healer

The organization of French grammar and vocabulary coincides with the 'natural' ordering of time and space

Here we would expect the language to provide a linguistic expression for every distinct idea and reserve only one idea for each linguistic expression. On these counts it is very hard to demonstrate that French fares better (or worse) than any other language. Indeed, don't the speakers of most languages consider their mother tongue to provide the most natural vehicle for their thoughts?

Since there is no limit to the ideas human beings are likely to have, we can be sure that there will be plenty of ideas for which French has no neatly coded expression. The French past-tense system, for instance, fails to distinguish between 'I sang' and 'I have sung' – a distinction which we in English find indispensable. They have the same word for 'sheep' and 'mutton', for 'ox' and 'beef'. Similarly, there are plenty of words in French which have more than one meaning (e.g. *poser* = (1) put down, (2) ask [a question], (3) pose [for a picture]), and a large number of words which all sound the same (e.g. *ver* = 'worm', *verre* = 'glass', *vert* = 'green', *vair* = 'a type of fur', *vers* = 'towards', *vers* = 'verse'). All of these breach the 'rule' of clarity and are potential sources of ambiguity. Indeed, one of the principal sources of jokes in French is the pun:

e.g. *Napoleon*: 'Ma sacrée toux' (= My bloody cough!)
     Dim officer takes this to mean 'Massacrez tout!' (= Massacre everything!), so liquidates the entire population of the village.

French is a lucid language

It was Rivarol who declared that 'What is not clear is not French.' Well, on this count there must be millions of deprived people living and working in France with no language to call their own. Some might not be surprised if the unlettered masses produce jumbled and confused 'non-French', but even the educated elite, even those people whose business is style, have their problems:

Donner à l'analyse du style une configuration épistémique plus rigoureuse que celle qui consiste actuellement à remettre en circulation des concepts détramés et effilochés par l'usage, qui – dans les perspectives trop positivistes d'une extension réitérée de la rhétorique et de la 'linguistique du discours' aux actes de parole ou à la pragmatique – cherche à réduire l'analyse à des inventaires technologiques: tel est le dessein . . .

Giving to the analysis of style a more rigorous epistemic configuration than the one which currently consists of putting back into circulation concepts slackened and frayed by usage, which – in the over-positivistic perspective of a repeated extension of rhetoric and 'discourse linguistics' to speech-acts or pragmatics – seeks to reduce analysis to technological inventories: such is the purpose . . .

The idea which people seem to find very hard to grasp is that languages cannot possess good or bad qualities: no language system can ever be shown to be clearer or more logical (or more beautiful or more ugly) than any other language system. Where differences of clarity and logic are to be found is not in the language itself but in the abilities of different users of the language to handle it effectively. Some French speakers produce utterances which are marvellous in their lucidity, while others can always be relied upon to produce impenetrable gibberish – but it is the speakers who deserve our praise or blame, not the language.

How is it that so obviously mythical an idea as the logicality of French has taken such strong root in France and to some extent among her neighbours? The external perceptions of French are not too hard to explain – they seem to be bound up with the national stereotypes which developed in Europe a century ago and which are sadly still around today. Italian became a 'musical language', no doubt because of its association in the minds of non-Italians with Italian opera; German became a 'harsh, guttural language' because of Prussian militarism; Spanish became a 'romantic language' because of bull-fighters and flamenco dancing; French almost inevitably became a 'logical language' thanks to prestigious philosophers like Descartes, whose mode of thinking was felt to contrast sharply with that of the 'pragmatic English'.

But why should the French have taken on board the myth of logic and clarity so fully themselves? Here the answer perhaps lies in the important role played in the development of French culture by the standard language. A standard language is a set of ideas about what constitutes the best form of a language, the form which everyone ought to imitate.

When the notion of standard language started to gain ground in France in the sixteenth century, the question of what made the 'best form' of French better than the rest was a relatively simple one: the 'best French was the best, because it was spoken by the best people (i.e. the King and his Court).' In the age of absolutism established in the seventeenth and eighteenth centuries, hitching linguistic norms to aristocratic fashion came to be regarded as too crude and too fragile a basis upon which to fix the standard language. What constituted the 'best French' had to be anchored in something more rational and permanent: so the powers-that-be convinced themselves that 'the French (of the best people) was the best, because it corresponded the most closely to the timeless dictates of logic and clarity.' Thereafter, only 'the best French' – those uses of French which complied with what people then considered clear and logical – was deemed worthy of the label 'French' at all. Hence Rivarol's circular slogan 'What is not clear is not French.'

But things did not stop there. In 1793 the Revolutionaries decapitated their king and the nation desperately needed a new symbol for its identity to ensure solidarity within France and distinctiveness without. The French standard language was roped in for the job. It is not uncommon, even today, to hear French people speak of 'Her Majesty the French language'. Since the French language is the language of reason and logic, any French person who uses it improperly must be cognitively defective, irrational, even mad. Since the French language is now the symbol of the nation, failure to use the national language and even failure to use it 'properly' makes you a traitor to the national cause. Indeed, it is still widely believed that to speak French badly, to break the rules of French grammar or to make frequent use of foreign words is to be in some way unpatriotic. In 1980 the politician Raymond Barre is reported to have said, 'The first of the fundamental values of our civilization is the correct usage of our language. There is among young people a moral and civic virtue in the loyal practice of French.'

It is easy for Anglo-Saxons, for whom language is not normally a fundamental element of national identity, to be patronizing about the French agonizing over the intrinsic qualities and status of their language. However, they would be unwise to underestimate the capacity of language to generate national solidarity in the struggle for economic and cultural dominance which permanently characterizes international affairs. This is particularly so in France. French politicians know this and exploit it to powerful effect.

Sources and further reading

For a general overview of myths about language circulating in France, see Marina Yaguello, *Catalogue des idées reçues sur la langue* (Paris: Seuil, 1988). For a collection of studies focusing specifically on the question of the clarity of French, see the journal *Langue française* 75 (1987), Marc Wilmet (ed.). The question is discussed in English in 'The myth of clarity', *The Times Literary Supplement*, 4.6.62.

English Spelling is Kattastroffik

Edward Carney

BRITISH WORKER: *I can't work today. I've got diarrhoea.*
AMERICAN BOSS: *Diarrhea? That's dreadful. You could have sent me a sick note.*
BRITISH WORKER: *But I can't spell it.*

Not many people *can* spell this particular word either in the British or in the somewhat simplified American fashion. Yet if you know how an English word is pronounced and roughly what it means, you ought to be able to write it down without much trouble. If you find that you can't do that, then the writing system may well seem to be at fault.

However, 'catastrophic' is a severe word. Before rushing to condemn the whole system, you ought to see what English spelling sets out to do and the extent to which it is consistent in doing it.

In looking at spelling we need to keep sounds and letters quite separate. So letters are cited in angled brackets and symbols for speech-sounds are put between slant lines. The letters <said> spell /sed/ and <text> spells /tekst/.

People often foul things up when talking about spelling because they do not differentiate between letters and sounds. It is best to use 'vowel' and 'consonant' only for sounds. The words *fight, cry, shop, axe, coin, caught* each contain two consonants and one vowel.

If you want to talk about letters then say 'vowel letter' and 'consonant letter'. Unusual re-spellings or mistakes are marked with an asterisk: *<stoopid>, *<langwidge>.

How the alphabet copes

The myth that there are 'five vowels' in English refers to the vowel letters <a, e, i, o, u> of the roman alphabet. Depending on your accent, you will find about twenty vowels in English. Try collecting them by changing the vowel sound in a series of otherwise identical-sounding words, noting each new vowel that turns up. If you start with, say, *lick*, you can change the vowel sound and get a different word *lack*. Without bothering about the spelling, carry on ringing the changes of sound and you will turn up *lock, luck, leak, lake, like*. You will find the vowel of *leak* again in *feel*, but that frame will give you some new ones, as in *fell, full, foil, fowl, foal, fall*, and so on in other frames. Some twenty-four consonant sounds can be found by the same method: *bet, debt, get, jet, let, met, net, pet, set, vet, wet, yet*. A different frame will give you some new ones in *sheaf, sheath, sheathe, sheet*, and even *chic* (or *sheik*). Some less common consonants will be quite hard to find, such as the middle one in *measure*.

In a Garden-of-Eden alphabetic writing system, you would have a single letter for each speech-sound and one speech-sound for each single letter. Large numbers of English words appear to follow this strict pattern: *best, dispel, dividend, film, frog, help, jam, limit, map, profit, rob, splint, tendril, win, yet*, etc. But if we look further, we soon see that too many speech-sounds are chasing too few letters.

Most consonants, at least some of the time, may have a single-letter 'alphabetic' spelling: <b, d, f, g, h, j, l, m, n, p, r, s, t, v, w, y, z>; /k/ has a choice of <c> or <k>. But there is often 'divergence', where one speech-sound has several different spellings and one spelling may stand for different speech-sounds. In spite of the available single-letter spelling <f>, the consonant at the beginning of *foot* has more complex spellings in *physics, enough, offer*. The <s> in *easy* represents /z/, the <u> in *quick* represents /w/ and the <f> in *of* represents /v/. The consonant at the beginning of *yet, yellow* also comes pre-packed as part of the vowel spelt <u(e)> in *cue, cute, pure*. The most divergent consonant is /k/, which has different spellings in *catch, chemist, back, acclaim, chukker, key, quay, quite, Iraq* and as part of the /ks/ in *axe*.

Six consonants do not have a single-letter spelling of their own and require at least two letters, such as <sh> or <ch>. These are the consonants found in the middle of the following words: *method*, *bother*, *wishing*, *measure*, *patches* and the consonant represented by <ng> in *singer* when no actual /g/ is pronounced.

Vowel markers

Five pairs of vowels can have single-letter spellings: <a> in *scrap*, *scraping*, <e> in *met*, *meter*, <i> in *pip*, *piper*, <o> in *cop*, *coping*, <u> in *rub*, *ruby*. There is also <y> in *cryptic*, *cry*, which duplicates the <i> spellings. The examples given in each pair represent a 'short' and a 'long' vowel.

For this letter-sharing to work, 'markers' are needed in some contexts to tell you which value the letter has. To get the long value of <a> in a single-syllable word, you have to add a marker <-e>, as in *scrape*. To get the short value before a suffix beginning with a vowel like <-ing>, you double a final consonant letter, as in *scrapping*. So, with this marking, a single vowel letter can be used with two values in *scrap*, *scrape*, *scrapping*, *scraping*.

Four consonants have unusual doubling. The normal doubling of /k/ in native words is <ck>: *stoking*, *stocking*; *baker*, *backer*. The consonant at the end of *beach* and *batch* has <ch> as its 'single' spelling and <tch> as its 'doubled' spelling. Similarly we have <g(e)> as a 'single' spelling and <dg(e)> as a 'doubled' spelling in *cadge*, *cage*. A doubled <vv> occurs only in slang words: *navvy*, *luvvies*, *revving*. So the vowel difference in words such as *level*, *seven*, *devil* and *fever*, *even*, *evil* is not marked.

Keeping a spelling constant

Some words are made up of several recognizable building blocks. The word *reason* is a single unit, while *un+reason+able+ness* consists of four. The *son* bit is not such a unit. English spelling often tries to give each of these building blocks a constant spelling. A good example is the verbal ending <-ed>. This sounds quite different in *wished, begged*, and *wanted*. If you think that they would be better spelt phonetically as *<wisht>, *<begd>, you are losing the advantage of a constant spelling for the regular past-tense ending.

You may think it awkward to have /s/ spelt differently in *sent* and *cent*. That may be, but the <c> spelling of both /k/ in *electric* and /s/ in *electricity* keeps the spelling of that unit constant.

The best examples of this principle are the long and short spellings of single vowel letters seen in word pairs such as:

atrocious – atrocity	female – feminine	omen – ominous
austere – austerity	grateful – gratitude	reside – residual
chaste – chastity	legal – legislate	sole – solitude
crime – criminal	mine – mineral	supreme – supremacy

In these pairs the basic long vowel is shortened when it comes three syllables from the end of the word. These shortened vowels do not require marking with a double consonant letter as *<omminous>, *<minneral> or *<sollitude>.

Keeping a constant spelling may involve the use of so-called 'silent' letters. The <g> does not represent /g/ in *sign*, but it does in derived forms *resignation, signal, signature, signify*. Similarly we have *malign, malignant*. Changing to *<sine>, *<maline> would spoil the visual link. Should we keep the <w> of *two* because *twenty, twin, between* are remotely related? Should *shepherd* be re-spelt as *<sheppard>, a regularized spelling when used as a name?

On the other hand the <g> of *gnarled, gnat, gnash, gnaw, gnome* and the <k> of *knee, knife, knight, knock, know, knuckle* are quite empty letters. They are the debris of history and are never pronounced in any derived word (except for *acknowledge*). It would be no loss to change to *<narled>, *<nat>, *<nife>, *<nuckle>, etc.

Other markers

There are other important markers. The <-e> in *bathe, breathe, loathe, wreathe* not only marks the vowel as long but marks the last consonant as 'voiced' rather than the 'voiceless' one in *bath, breath, loath, wreath*. Other examples are *lathe, lithe, swathe*. *Mouth* and *smooth* used as verbs lack this marking.

The marker <-e> in *browse, copse, lapse, please, tease, tense* is used to prevent confusion with the plural forms *brows, cops, laps, pleas, teas, tens*. It marks the *browse* group as single units and as such is called 'lexical <-e>'.

Some marking is needed to sort out the two distinct consonants represented by <g>. Before <a, o, u> we have /g/, as in *gap, got, gum* and the consonant spelt <j> in *jam* before <i, e> in *gin, gem*. The problem is that there are some exceptions with /g/ before <i, e>: *gear, geese, get, giddy, gild, gilt, gimmick, girl, give*. Some words however have used the letter <u> as a marker for /g/ in *guess, guest, guide, guild, guilt, guise, guitar*. Its use is not very consistent, since *guard, guarantee* do not need any <u> marker (cf. *garden*).

Look-alikes and sound-alikes

Words spelt the same but pronounced differently are called homographs: <minute> may be an adjective ('a really minute insect') or a noun ('half a minute'). A *minute steak* has to be interpreted by the reader: either a very small steak or one cooked for a minute.

Words pronounced the same but spelt differently are called homophones: <vain>, <vane>, <vein>, or <foul>, <fowl>, or <meat>, <meet>, <mete>. These variant vowel spellings clearly make it harder for the writer, but it is often claimed that such divergence is not always a bad thing for the reader, since different words should look different on the printed page.

Even so, a good number of words are both homographs and homophones: sounding the same and looking the same. These are sometimes called homonyms. For instance, *hamper* represents two completely different unrelated words: either 'a basket' or 'to hinder'. *Quarry* means either 'a stone quarry' or 'a hunted animal'. You will find two or more very different words sharing each of the following forms: *bark, bellows, bound, cricket, fine, firm, fit, flat, hail, last, leaves, pants, plane, quail, rest, rose, stable*. Check in a good dictionary if in doubt. The intended sense is usually obvious from the context. If spelling reform reduced divergence, it would clearly add to the number of such homonyms: 'a weather vane', 'a *vane in the wrist' and 'very *vane'.

A muddy sort of vowel

A vowel may be weakened by lack of stress. Unless you are speaking very formally the highlighted vowel letters in the following words all spell the same indistinct /ə/ sound: *about, asparagus, author, caravan, courageous, driver, polite, together*. This obscure vowel has borrowed the name 'schwa' from Hebrew. As you can see, the spelling of /ə/ varies widely, since it reflects what the vowel would be in a stressed context. You find /ə/ equally in *organ, political, president*, but the spelling is prompted by the stressed vowels of *organic, politics, presidential*. The spelling of the basic units is constant.

Clever stuff

Words borrowed from French have sometimes been altered by anxious academics looking beyond the French spelling to the distant Latin original. The words *debt, doubt*, were medieval borrowings of French *dette* 'debt', *doute* 'doubt' without a <b>. The 'silent' <b> was inserted in the sixteenth century to resemble the original Latin *debitum, dubitare*, and to draw attention to the shared meaning of related English words derived from the same roots, such as *debit, dubitative*.

Before the eighteenth century, *subtle* was generally spelt <suttle>, just like regular *scuttle*, even by authors such as Milton, a well-known

Latin scholar. In spite of this the present spelling with an empty <b> was adopted to match Latin *subtilis*, though the <b> has never been pronounced in English.

Such interference is often inconsistent. The <p> of *receipt* links it to *receptacle, reception*, but *deceit* lacks a <p>, in spite of *deception*. The <c> spelling of the early French loan *grocer* is a regular English spelling (*racer, slicer*), so why not have *gross* spelt *<groce> on the lines of *race, truce, slice*? As it is, *gross* is the only English word in which <oss> does not sound as it does in *boss, cross, doss, dross, floss*. Ironically, the regular *<groce> was a common medieval spelling that did not survive.

A similar mismatch is the French <gn> spelling of *align, alignment*. The base form in English is <line> and not, as in French, *<ligne>. However, some dictionaries do allow the common-sense spelling <aline>, <alinement>. The <b> of *crumb, crumby* is only pronounced in *crumble*. Interestingly, when used as slang, *crummy* will have a straight phonetic spelling. *Dummy* likewise comes from *dumb*.

A system of subsystems

The Old English of the Anglo-Saxons has given us our basic stock of words: *life, death, earth, heaven, sun, moon, day, night, black, white, broad, narrow, teach, learn, seek, find, eat, drink, food, meat, fire, wood, tree, eye, knee, hand, foot* and so on.

Since medieval times English has adopted cultural loanwords from French. The early ones included *attach, certain, chance, conquer, courage, language, money, place, pleasant, royal, strange, sure, tender, value*, and even a word as common now as *very*, which at first meant 'true'.

Modern loanwords from French come with their present French spelling and a close approximation to French pronunciation: *collage, entourage, piquant, pirouette*.

Technical terms for use in science are often derived from Latin or Greek. *Aqueduct, subaquatic* are Latinate counterparts in meaning to ordinary English *waterway, underwater*. Similarly, Greek elements make up scientific terms such as *photosynthesis, polyglot, pyromania*.

The <-rrh(o)ea> of *diarrhea* ('through-flow') recurs in other Greek-based words such as *catarrh* ('down-flow'), *seborrhoea* ('grease-flow'). Scientists have to learn a mini-language of such elements. When such terms escape into common use they often cause spelling problems for the ordinary person, as we saw at the outset.

That leaves a whole array of loanwords that are variously 'exotic': *kayak* is from Eskimo, *felucca* is from Arabic by way of Italian. The now familiar *tobacco* comes from Arawak, an American-Indian language.

These various subsystems are often marked by their own peculiar spelling correspondences. If you know a *yucca* to be an exotic plant, you will not spell it *<yucker>. The <ch> of *chief*, an early French loan, has the same sound as in native *cheap*, *cheese*. The modern loan *chef* retains its present French value of <ch> (like the <sh> of *shop*), as do *chauffeur*, *charade*. The spelling is not altered to *<shef>. This same <ch> will also spell /k/ in Greek-based words such as *character*, *chemist*, *synchronic*. Similarly, <ph> is a 'Greek' spelling for /f/, as in *diaphragm*, *philosophy*, *phobia*, *symphony*.

Borrowing foreign spellings along with foreign loanwords is not the only way of doing it. In Swedish, for example, foreign loans are usually spelt with ordinary Swedish spelling. So French loans *coiffure*, *pirouette* are spelt in Swedish as <koaffyr> and <piruett>. If we decided to impose a single uniform system of regular alphabetic spellings and ignore the origin of words, markers of cultural origin would be lost. Would that matter?

Different speakers, different problems

English spelling has to cater for a wide range of English accents, which differ in their goodness of fit with present spelling conventions. If you pronounce <w> and <wh> the same in *witch*, *which*; *weather*, *whether*; *wine*, *whine*; then you have to learn by rote which individual words have <wh->. If, as in much of southern England, you pronounce *court*, *cores*, *floor*, *formerly*, *source* without an /r/ and hence the same as *caught*, *cause*, *flaw*, *formally*, *sauce*, you have to learn which individual words have an <r> and which do not. Most Scottish, Irish and American speakers have kept their /r/ in all positions and so have a spelling advantage here.

The price of history

The spelling system has to cater as best it can for phonetic differences between speakers. If people were encouraged to spell as they spoke, there would emerge a number of different written dialects of English.

Like flies in amber, English spelling has preserved a continuous record of cultural activity by borrowing foreign spelling conventions along with the borrowed words. The spelling of *phlegm* tells you that it is a scientific term and that it is related to *phlegmatic*. But for those who are struggling towards literacy, it might be better to spell it *<flem>.

Sources and further reading

For detailed references on topics such as spelling reform, spelling and dialect, the spelling of names, types of spelling mistake, homophones and homographs and an analysis in detail of spelling correspondences, see Edward Carney, *A Survey of English Spelling* (London: Routledge, 1994). A short practical textbook by the same author is *English Spelling* (London: Routledge, 1997) in the series Language Workbooks.

Women Talk Too Much

Janet Holmes

Do women talk more than men? Proverbs and sayings in many languages express the view that women are always talking:

Women's tongues are like lambs' tails – they are never still. –English

The North Sea will sooner be found wanting in water than a woman at a loss for words. –Jutlandic

The woman with active hands and feet, marry her, but the woman with overactive mouth, leave well alone. –Maori

Some suggest that while women talk, men are silent patient listeners.

When both husband and wife wear pants it is not difficult to tell them apart – he is the one who is listening. –American

Nothing is so unnatural as a talkative man or a quiet woman. –Scottish

Others indicate that women's talk is not valued but is rather considered noisy, irritating prattle:

Where there are women and geese there's noise. –Japanese

Indeed, there is a Japanese character which consists of three instances of the character for the concept 'woman' and which translates as 'noisy'! My favourite proverb, because it attributes not noise but rather power to the woman speaker is this Chinese one:

The tongue is the sword of a woman and she never lets it become rusty.

So what are the facts? Do women dominate the talking time? Do men struggle to get a word in edgewise, as the stereotype suggests?

The evidence

Despite the widespread belief that women talk more than men, most of the available evidence suggests just the opposite. When women and men are together, it is the men who talk most. Two Canadian researchers, Deborah James and Janice Drakich, reviewed sixty-three studies which examined the amount of talk used by American women and men in different contexts. Women talked more than men in only two studies.

In New Zealand, too, research suggests that men generally dominate the talking time. Margaret Franken compared the amount of talk used by female and male 'experts' assisting a female TV host to interview well-known public figures. In a situation where each of three interviewers was entitled to a third of the interviewers' talking time, the men took more than half on every occasion.

I found the same pattern analysing the number of questions asked by participants in one hundred public seminars. In all but seven, men dominated the discussion time. Where the numbers of women and men present were about the same, men asked almost two-thirds of the questions during the discussion. Clearly women were not talking more than men in these contexts.

Even when they hold influential positions, women sometimes find it hard to contribute as much as men to a discussion. A British company appointed four women and four men to the eight most highly paid management positions. The managing director commented that the men often patronized the women and tended to dominate meetings:

I had a meeting with a [female] sales manager and three of my [male] directors once . . . it took about two hours. She only spoke once and one of my fellow directors cut across her and said 'What Anne is trying to say Roger is . . .' and I think that about sums it up. He knew better than Anne what she was trying to say, and she never got anything said.

There is abundant evidence that this pattern starts early. Many researchers have compared the relative amounts that girls and boys contribute to classroom talk. In a wide range of communities, from kindergarten through primary, secondary and tertiary education, the same pattern recurs – males dominate classroom talk. So on this evidence we must conclude that the stereotype of the garrulous woman reflects sexist prejudice rather than objective reality.

Looking for an explanation

Why is the reality so different from the myth? To answer this question, we need to go beyond broad generalizations and look more carefully at the patterns identified. Although some teachers claim that boys are 'by nature more spirited and less disciplined', there is no evidence to suggest that males are biologically programmed to talk more than females. It is much more likely that the explanation involves social factors.

What is the purpose of the talk?
One relevant clue is the fact that talk serves different functions in different contexts. Formal public talk is often aimed at informing people or persuading them to agree to a particular point of view (e.g.

political speeches, television debates, radio interviews, public lectures, etc.). Public talk is often undertaken by people who wish to claim or confirm some degree of public status. Effective talk in public and in the media can enhance your social status – as politicians and other public performers know well. Getting and holding the floor is regarded as desirable, and competition for the floor in such contexts is common. (There is also some risk, of course, since a poor performance can be damaging.)

Classroom research suggests that more talk is associated with higher social status or power. Many studies have shown that teachers (regardless of their gender) tend to talk for about two-thirds of the available time. But the boys dominate the relatively small share of the talking time that remains for pupils. In this context, where talk is clearly valued, it appears that the person with most status has the right to talk most. The boys may therefore be asserting a claim to higher status than the girls by appropriating the majority of the time left for pupil talk.

Doonesbury   BY GARRY TRUDEAU

The way women and men behave in formal meetings and seminars provides further support for this explanation. Evidence collected by

American, British and New Zealand researchers shows that men dominate the talking time in committee meetings, staff meetings, seminars and task-oriented decision-making groups. If you are sceptical, use a stopwatch to time the amount of talk contributed by women and men at political and community meetings you attend. This explanation proposes that men talk more than women in public, formal contexts because they perceive participating and verbally contributing in such contexts as an activity which enhances their status, and men seem to be more concerned with asserting status and power than women are.

By contrast, in more private contexts, talk usually serves interpersonal functions. The purpose of informal or intimate talk is not so much status enhancement as establishing or maintaining social contact with others, making social connections, developing and reinforcing friendships and intimate relationships. Interestingly, the few studies which have investigated informal talk have found that there are fewer differences in the amount contributed by women and men in these contexts (though men still talked more in nearly a third of the informal studies reviewed by Deborah James and Janice Drakich). Women, it seems, are willing to talk more in relaxed social contexts, especially where the talk functions to develop and maintain social relationships.

Another piece of evidence that supports this interpretation is the *kind* of talk women and men contribute in mixed-sex discussions. Researchers analysing the functions of different utterances have found that men tend to contribute more information and opinions, while women contribute more agreeing, supportive talk, more of the kind of talk that encourages others to contribute. So men's talk tends to be more referential or informative, while women's talk is more supportive and facilitative.

Overall, then, women seem to use talk to develop personal relationships and maintain family connections and friendships more often than to make claims to status or to directly influence others in public contexts. Of course, there are exceptions, as Margaret Thatcher, Benazir Bhutto and Jenny Shipley demonstrate. But, until recently, many women seem not to have perceived themselves as appropriate contributors to public, formal talk.

In New Zealand we identified another context where women contributed more talk than men. Interviewing people to collect samples of talk for linguistic analysis, we found that women were much more likely than men (especially young men) to be willing to talk to us at length. For example, Miriam Meyerhoff asked a group of ten young people to describe a picture to a female and to a male interviewer. It was made quite clear to the interviewees that the more speech they produced the better. In this situation, the women contributed significantly more speech than the men, both to the male and to the female interviewer.

In the private but semi-formal context of an interview, then, women contributed more talk than men. Talk in this context could not be seen as enhancing the status of the people interviewed. The interviewers were young people with no influence over the interviewees. The explanation for the results seems to be that the women were being more cooperative than the men in a context where more talk was explicitly sought by the interviewer.

Social confidence

If you know a lot about a particular topic, you are generally more likely to be willing to contribute to a discussion about it. So familiarity or expertise can also affect the amount a person contributes to a particular discussion. In one interesting study the researcher supplied particular people with extra information, making them the 'experts' on the topic to be discussed. Regardless of gender, these 'experts' talked more in the subsequent discussions than their uninformed conversational partners (though male 'experts' still used more talking time in conversation with uninformed women than female 'experts' did with uninformed men).

Looking at people's contributions to the discussion section of seminars, I found a similar effect from expertise or topic familiarity. Women were more likely to ask questions and make comments when the topic was one they could claim expert knowledge about. In a small seminar on the current state of the economy, for instance, several women economists who had been invited to attend contributed to the discussion, making this one of the very few seminars where women's contributions exceeded men's.

Another study compared the relative amount of talk of spouses. Men dominated the conversations between couples with traditional gender roles and expectations, but when the women were associated with a feminist organization they tended to talk more than their husbands. So feminist women were more likely to challenge traditional gender roles in interaction.

It seems possible that both these factors – expert status and feminist philosophy – have the effect of developing women's social confidence. This explanation also fits with the fact that women tend to talk more with close friends and family, when women are in the majority, and also when they are explicitly invited to talk (in an interview, for example).

Perceptions and implications

If social confidence explains the greater contributions of women in some social contexts, it is worth asking why girls in school tend to contribute less than boys. Why should they feel unconfident in the classroom? Here is the answer which one sixteen-year-old gave:

Sometimes I feel like saying that I disagree, that there are other ways of looking at it, but where would that get me? My teacher thinks I'm showing off, and the boys jeer. But if I pretend I don't understand, it's very different. The teacher is sympathetic and the boys are helpful. They really respond if they can show YOU how it is done, but there's nothing but 'aggro' if you give any signs of showing THEM how it is done.

Talking in class is often perceived as 'showing off', especially if it is girl-talk. Until recently, girls have preferred to keep a low profile rather than attract negative attention.

Teachers are often unaware of the gender distribution of talk in their classrooms. They usually consider that they give equal amounts of attention to girls and boys, and it is only when they make a tape recording that they realize that boys are dominating the interactions. Dale Spender, an Australian feminist who has been a strong advocate of female rights in this area, noted that teachers who tried to restore the balance by deliberately 'favouring' the girls were astounded to find that despite their efforts they continued to devote more time to the boys in their classrooms. Another study reported that a male science teacher who managed to create an atmosphere in which girls and boys contributed more equally to discussion felt that he was devoting 90 per cent of his attention to the girls. And so did his male pupils. They complained vociferously that the girls were getting too much talking time.

In other public contexts, too, such as seminars and debates, when women and men are deliberately given an equal amount of the highly valued talking time, there is often a perception that they are getting more than their fair share. Dale Spender explains this as follows:

The talkativeness of women has been gauged in comparison not with men but with silence. *Women have not been judged on the grounds of whether they talk more than men, but of whether they talk more than silent women.*

In other words, if women talk at all, this may be perceived as 'too much' by men who expect them to provide a silent, decorative background in many social contexts. This may sound outrageous, but think about how you react when precocious children dominate the talk at an adult party. As women begin to make inroads into formerly 'male' domains such as business and professional contexts, we should not be surprised to find that their contributions are not always perceived positively or even accurately.

Conclusion

We have now reached the conclusion that the question 'Do women talk more than men?' can't be answered with a straight 'yes' or 'no'. The answer is rather, 'It all depends.' It depends on many different factors, including the social context in which the talk is taking place, the kind of talk involved and the relative social confidence of the speakers, which is affected by such things as their social roles (e.g. teacher, host, interviewee, wife) and their familiarity with the topic.

It appears that men generally talk more in formal, public contexts where informative and persuasive talk is highly valued, and where talk is generally the prerogative of those with some societal status and has the potential for increasing that status. Women, on the other hand, are more likely to contribute in private, informal interactions, where talk more often functions to maintain relationships, and in other situations where for various reasons they feel socially confident.

Finally, and most radically, we might question the assumption that more talk is always a good thing. 'Silence is golden,' says the proverb, and there are certainly contexts in all cultures where silence is more appropriate than talk, where words are regarded as inadequate vehicles for feelings, or where keeping silent is an expression of appreciation or respect. Sometimes it is the silent participants who are the powerful players. In some contexts the strong silent male is an admired stereotype. However, while this is true, it must be recognized that talk is very highly valued in western culture. It seems likely, then, that as long as holding the floor is equated with influence, the complexities of whether women or men talk most will continue to be a matter for debate.

Sources and further reading

For more detailed information including more details about the examples discussed, see the following sources: Deborah James and Janice Drakich, 'Understanding gender differences in amount of talk' in *Gender and Conversational Interaction*, Deborah Tannen (ed.) (Oxford: Oxford University Press, 1993, pp. 281–312); Janet Holmes, *Women, Men and Politeness* (London: Longman, 1995, chs. 2 and 6); Dale Spender, *Man Made Language* (London: Routledge and Kegan Paul, 1980); and Dale Spender and Elizabeth Sarah (eds.), *Learning to Lose* (London: The Women's Press, 1982).

Some Languages
are Harder than Others

Lars-Gunnar Andersson

Many people speak of languages as easy or difficult, meaning that it is easy or difficult to learn these languages. People do not usually talk about their mother tongues as being easy or difficult for them as native speakers to use. Swedish schoolchildren may say that English is much easier than German because English does not have as much grammar (see also Myth 10: Some Languages Have No Grammar). Immigrants can be heard saying that English, Swedish, German or some other language is quite difficult. Linguists prefer not to comment on such matters globally. There is, they would say, no single scale from easy to difficult, and degree of difficulty can be discussed on many levels.

The difficulty of learning a language as a foreign language refers to some kind of relative difficulty: how hard is it to get there from here? The real question posed here, though, is whether some languages are simpler than others in some absolute sense, in terms of their own systems rather than in terms of some external perspective. It is quite obvious that it is easier for a Swede to learn Norwegian than Polish. For a Czech it is easier to learn Polish than Norwegian. Swedish and Norwegian are similar because they are closely related linguistically and also because they have existed in close cultural contact for several centuries. Correspondingly, the Slavic languages Czech and Polish are close to each other, as are the Bantu languages Zulu and Xhosa in South Africa and the Dravidian languages Tamil and Telegu in southern India. This means that if you have English as your mother tongue, it is easier to learn Germanic languages like Dutch and German than it would be to learn Slavic languages like Polish and Russian or Turkic languages like Kazakh and Tatar. The major reason for this is that the vocabularies have so many similarities in both form and content in the related languages.

Let us look at the components of our linguistic knowledge, and let us assume that our knowledge of a language consists of the following three parts: grammar, vocabulary and rules of usage. This means that if you have English as your first language, you have an English grammar in your head. This grammar makes your pronunciation and your word order similar to that of other English speakers. You also have an English vocabulary at your disposal. We don't always find the right word when we speak, but very often we do (compare how hard it can be to find the right word when speaking a foreign language). You also have a number of rules of usage at your disposal. These rules tell you when to speak and when to keep quiet, how to address a person, how to ask questions and how to conduct a telephone conversation.

The difficult thing about learning a language is the vocabulary, whether learning one's native language or learning a foreign language. I make this claim even though I realize that millions of foreign-language learners have cursed the three genders and four cases of German grammar and the inflection of the French auxiliaries. Still, vocabulary takes longer to learn than either of the other facets mentioned. Each individual word is not difficult to learn, but when it is a matter of thousands of words, it does take a lot of time. We learn the grammar of our native language before we start school, but we work on our vocabulary as long as we live. Vocabulary is, then, the most difficult part and that which takes the longest time to learn. In the absolute sense, a language with few words should be easier to learn than one with many, but we cannot look at it that way. We need words to express our thoughts, and with fewer words some thoughts will be harder to express. Nobody learns all the words in a language, not even in his or her native language. Nor can anyone specify exactly how many words there are in a language; it is even difficult to define exactly what a word is. But to put things into perspective, we can say that modern dictionaries for English, German and other languages contain approximately 100,000 words.

The term 'rules of usage' refers to a number of things, for example rules for how and when one should speak and rules for who gets the floor in various social situations. The principle is probably that increased cultural proximity leads to increasingly similar rules of usage. Let's look at an example of this line of thought. For example, the vocabulary of Dutch is much easier for an English speaker than that of Irish or Welsh: so many Dutch words closely resemble English ones because these languages are so closely related. On the other hand the rules of usage are probably equally simple (or hard) in Dutch and Irish, and this is due to the cultural similarities of the Western European countries.

In the absolute sense, a language without complicated rules for politeness and indirect styles of expression should be easier to learn. Let's look at an example. A British lecturer says, 'Are you sure the baby will be all right in here?' to a Swedish student who has brought her baby along to a lecture. The student replies 'Sure, no problem,' but the lecturer probably intended the question as a request for the student to leave the room with the baby. This sort of misunderstanding is not uncommon when people from different cultures communicate and can be explained by different rules of usage. An easy language ought to be one with few rules for indirectness and a simple system for expressing politeness. In most of Europe, there are pronouns of power and solidarity (*du-Sie* in German, *tu-vous* in French and *ty-vy* in Russian). Nowadays, neither English nor Swedish makes use of this distinction. Thus, when it comes to form of address, English is simpler than either German or French. On the other hand, there might be other ways to signal social distance which are more subtle and, therefore, just as hard to learn, for example, choosing between *Johnnie*, *John*, *Smith*, *Mr Smith* and so on. It is difficult to say if there really are languages that are easier than others with respect to rules of usage. Natural languages are not only used to transfer information from one individual to another but also to indicate and to preserve social distinctions. And there are social distinctions in all societies. However, a language like Esperanto, which was constructed specifically to simplify communication between language groups, is in all likelihood easier than others in this particular respect.

For a language learner, the writing system and the orthography (rules for spelling) are major obstacles. Europeans have to spend a lot of time learning how to use the Arabic, Chinese or Japanese writing systems. These difficulties are not considered here, and the main argument for this is that the writing system and the spelling can be considered as external to the language. It is, in principle, possible to switch from one writing system to another without changing anything in the language structure. Turkish, for example, was written in the Arabic script before 1928. Since then it has been written in the Latin alphabet. This, of course, makes it much easier for anyone accustomed to the Latin alphabet. As far as spelling is concerned, an orthography following the principle that there should be a one-to-one correspondence between sounds and letters is simpler than one not meeting this condition. European languages with a written language history going back a thousand years or more have more complicated orthographies than languages which have only recently been reduced to writing. In making a new orthography, one would not invent mute letters, for example.

If we are looking for an absolute measure of linguistic simplicity, we should find it in the field of grammar. We can begin by considering the sound systems of languages. It must surely be the case that the fewer vowels, the fewer consonants and the simpler syllabic structure a language has, the simpler the sound system is. Hawaiian has thirteen distinctive sounds ('phonemes' in linguistic terminology), of which eight are consonants and five are vowels. Since the language also has strict rules about the syllable structure (almost all syllables have to consist of one consonant and one vowel in that order), the total number of possible syllables in the language is only 162. Compare English, where consonants can be grouped together both before and after the vowel as in *screams* and *splints*. Of all the languages of the world, Hawaiian has one of the simplest sound systems. At the other end of the scale we find the Khoisan languages (previously known as Bushman and Hottentot languages). According to a recently published description, !Xóõ (that is actually how it is spelt), a language spoken in Southern Botswana, has 156 phonemes, of which 78 are rather unusual sounds called clicks, 50 are ordinary consonants and 28 are vowels. Studies of other languages in the area have also arrived at phoneme counts of around 150. The sound systems of these languages are extremely complex. We can rest assured that the pronunciation of Hawaiian would be easier to learn than that of the Khoisan languages. We can also sum up by saying that it actually seems to make sense to place the languages of the world along a scale from simple sound systems to difficult. English takes a place near the middle of such a scale, where most of the languages of the world also crowd. Hence, most languages are equally difficult as far as the sound system is concerned, but there are some examples of considerably simpler and more difficult languages at this level.

There are classifications of the languages of the world according to how they deal with inflection and derivation, that is, patterns for constructing words by the addition of word elements ('morphemes' in linguistic terminology). A word such as *teachers* can be divided into the following morphemes *teach-er-s*, where *-er* is a derivational morpheme and *-s* an inflectional morpheme. We speak of analytic languages with little or no inflection and derivation and synthetic languages with a large degree of inflection and derivation. We can say that English is more analytic than Swedish and that Swedish is more analytic than German, but none of these languages are among the extreme cases. Vietnamese is extremely analytic and Greenlandic is extremely synthetic, just to mention two examples. In absolute terms one could say that analytic languages are easier than synthetic languages, and there are two arguments for this claim. Firstly, children always learn a more analytic version of their native language first; inflectional and derivational suffixes are learned later on. Secondly, pidgin languages from around the world are typically analytic. By pidgin languages we mean contact languages that arise or develop spontaneously. Most pidgin languages are found in the old European colonies around the world. One such language is Fanagalo, which has been used as a contact language between whites, blacks and coloureds in southern Africa since the nineteenth century, not least in the mining industry and in domestic services. Here are some examples from an introduction to the language. What we are interested in here is the grammatical structure of the sentences, not what they reveal about the social situation in pre-independent South Africa.

Wena   azi   lo golof?
You   know   the golf?
'Have you caddied before?'

Mina hayifuna   lo mampara mfan
I   not-want the useless   boy
'I don't want a useless boy.'

Yebo nkos, mina festklas   kedi
Yes Sir,   I   first-class caddie
'Yes, Sir, I'm a first-class caddie.'

Tata mabol, yena doti,   susa yena nga lo manzi
Take balls,   they dirty, wash them in the water
'These balls are dirty, clean them in water.'

There are several things making this language much simpler than any
of the languages from which it has been formed. *Mina* means both *I*
and *me*, *yena* both *they* and *them*. To express possession, *ga-* is placed
before the word: *gamina* 'mine' and *gayena* 'their'. The plural is always
formed by placing *ma-* in front of the word: *bol*, 'ball' and *mabol*,
'balls'. It is simpler to have one plural ending instead of several, as
English does. The definite article is invariably *lo*, which is easier than
having a number of different articles as in German, where there are
three genders with different articles (*der*, *die* and *das*) or French, with
two genders (*le* and *la*). The list of simple and general rules of the
language could be made much longer. The world's most famous
pidgin language speaker is Tarzan. When he says 'Me Tarzan, you
Jane,' he uses a simplified version of English. Since Tarzan has been
translated and published in several languages, we could travel around
the globe buying Tarzan magazines and in that way get an impression
of what people regard as simplified versions of their respective languages. A safe guess is that Tarzan speaks a more analytic version of
the language than his readership and in each case Tarzan is likely to
have fewer forms in his morphology than the readership.

One could, of course, object that pidgin languages are not real languages because nobody has them as a mother tongue. On the other hand, pidgin languages sometimes become the mother tongue of a group of people. They are then called creole languages. During the process of creolization, different complications in the grammar (as well as in the lexicon) will arise, but for a number of generations these creole languages will remain relatively simple. There is then good reason to believe that analytic languages are easier than synthetic. A more general conclusion could be that it is actually possible to speak of easier and harder languages with regard to grammar.

Once we look away from pidgins and creoles, which may be thought of as developing languages, we find another problem with talking about simplicity. Languages are not uniformly simple or difficult. We might think that Finnish is simpler than English because it has no articles (words corresponding to *a* and *the*); on the other hand, we might think it is more difficult than English because it has an elaborate system of inflections on nouns. Simplicity in one part of the language may be balanced by complexity in another part.

In fact, matters are less straightforward than even this suggests, because it is not necessarily the case that we can judge in any sensible way what is or is not simple. For example, some languages – Maori is one – allow only one adjective to modify a noun at a time. So, to translate the English *I saw a fat black cat*, you would have to say the equivalent of something like *I saw a fat cat. It was black.* Is the English system simpler because it uses fewer words? Or is the other system simpler because it has a less complex structure of modification? It is not clear that such questions can be meaningfully answered, and so not clear that we can give overall measurements of simplicity in syntax.

Considering what has been said above, the myth that some languages are harder than others is not merely a myth. In a fairly complicated way, and in certain respects, some languages are harder than others. Furthermore, there is no single scale for measuring simplicity in language; there are, at least, a handful of such scales. The real problems emerge when we try to figure out the possible trading relationships between the different scales. For example: does simplification on one scale lead to complication on another? Summing up: Some languages appear to be harder than others, but it is hard to explain exactly how and to what extent.

Sources and further reading

Many of the facts about the languages of the world have been taken from David Crystal's *The Cambridge Encyclopedia of Language* (Cambridge: Cambridge University Press, 1987). The Fanagalo sentences are taken from J. D. Bold's *Fanagalo: Phrase-Book, grammar and dictionary* (Pretoria: J. L. van Schaik, 15th edn, 1990). This book is referred to in L.-G. Andersson and T. Janson's *Languages in Botswana* (Gaborone: Longman, Botswana, 1997), from which most of the facts about African languages are taken. The technical terms used, such as 'phoneme', 'morpheme', 'orthography', 'analytic' and 'synthetic', can be found in most introductory books about linguistics.

Children Can't Speak or Write Properly Any More

James Milroy

For centuries now there have been recurrent complaints about the state of the English language. These complaints always seem to assume that the language is in decline and that this decline is associated with moral decline. Certain sections of society are normally held responsible for this decline, and one form that the complaint tradition can take is to associate linguistic decline with the use of the language by the younger generation. Young people, it is said, are liable to misuse the language, or not learn it properly: therefore, everything possible must be done to arrest this decline; for example, by tightening up in some way on language teaching in schools. In recent decades, there have been many complaints about what are believed to be declining educational standards, and in Britain such complaints have been fuelled by the government's proposals for a 'National Curriculum'. It is typically claimed that the schools are failing in their duty to teach children how to use English properly – both in speaking and in writing – and usually further claimed that this is due to modern teaching methods, which are said to be too permissive. Traditional methods, involving classroom drills and rote learning of correct spelling and grammar, are believed to have been in the past more effective in achieving and maintaining high standards of speaking and writing among children.

Although it is of course important that educational standards in schools should be carefully maintained, there is in reality nothing to suggest that today's youngsters are less competent at speaking and writing their native language than older generations of children were. Their ability to speak the language is just as good, and their ability to read and write it is, almost certainly, a great deal better on average.

Let's first consider the question of literacy. Is there any really persuasive evidence that literacy standards have declined?

In 1850 in England and Wales 31 per cent of bridegrooms and 46 per cent of brides could not write their names in the marriage register. By 1900 the percentage had declined to 3 per cent, and this reduction was largely a result of the 1870 Education Act, in which the British Government recognized the need for *functional literacy* among the working population and encouraged the teaching of the three Rs to everyone. Functional literacy means only the ability to read and write for practical purposes – understanding written messages from employers, for example, or writing simple instructions to other workers. It does not mean the ability to read Shakespeare with pleasure or partake in a high literary culture. If 97 per cent of the people could write their own names in 1900, it does not follow that they were all highly literate. It is likely that many of these people could not reliably spell 'difficult' words like *accommodate* and *desiccate*, keep up with international news in *The Times* or even write a fluent personal letter. The national aim had been to achieve functional literacy only, as this was the minimum necessary for the demands of a modern nation.

Those who complain today that standards of literacy are declining assume tacitly that there was a Golden Age in the past when our children, for the most part, could read and write more competently than they can today, and the complaints fit into a pattern of complaint literature that has been with us since the eighteenth century. In these complaints, linguistic decline is associated with moral decline, and this is the most powerful myth of all. For Jonathan Swift in 1712, it was the 'Licentiousness which entered with the Restoration [1660]' that infected our morals and then corrupted our language. In the nineteenth century, the poet G. M. Hopkins found 'this Victorian English . . . a bad business' – a language in decline. As for today, a headline in the *Observer* (4 August 1996) proclaims that 'written English is dying amid jargon, obscenity and ignorance,' and complaints of this kind can be found frequently in British and American newspapers. If we were to accept all this, we would have to accept that since the language has been declining since 1700, it must by now hardly be fit for use in writing a chapter in a book like this. Concern about our children's literacy and use of language generally is an aspect of this myth of moral and linguistic decline – as our children represent the future of the language, and the moral decline is often said to be associated with permissiveness in teaching method. There is, however, a tacit assumption in present-day complaints that things were better in the Good Old Days of strong moral discipline. There was a Golden Age when children could write much better than they can now.

Present-day complaints are never clear as to the Golden Age when children were more literate than they are now. When could it have been? Presumably, it cannot have been the eighteenth and nineteenth centuries, when – it seems – nearly 40 per cent of brides and bridegrooms could not write their own names. Perhaps the Golden Age envisaged is more recent than this: 1970? 1950? 1940? But again, when we look back at those times, it seems that much the same kinds of complaint about declining standards were current then. More importantly, it certainly does not seem that general standards of literacy were higher then than they are now.

In Britain the 1970s were the time of the *Black Papers*, edited by C. B. Cox and A. E. Dyson, which, among other things, drew attention to what were thought to be low standards of literacy in teacher-training colleges. These complaints made quite a strong impact, but from our present point of view, they suggest that we will not find the Golden Age in the 1970s. So could the Golden Age perhaps be the post-war period – approximately 1945–60? One important development in Britain around that time was the 1944 Education Act.

Before 1944 the population of England and Wales was not guaranteed a secondary education, and tertiary education was blocked to all but the rich and a few winners of university scholarships. A few people were highly literate and well versed in great literature, but not the majority. Higher education was, frankly, elitist and a preserve of the few. Indeed, during the recent debates about the National Curriculum, there were some letters to the newspapers questioning whether there really had been a Golden Age in those years. Here is one:

For some time I have been wondering if I was suffering from an acute shortage of memory. I remember many children in my primary school

*who were unable to read, and remember being shocked when called up
for national service to find myself in a platoon in which the majority of
members were illiterate . . . How consoling therefore to read . . . of Dirk
Bogarde's experience: 'The great majority of what was called the "Intake"
at Catterick Camp was, to my astonishment, illiterate.'*

*When exactly was the time that we hear so much about, when children
could all read and write and do everything so much better than today's
pupils? –Letter in the* Observer, *4 April 1993*

As national service ended in 1961, this is likely to refer to the 1950s.
The army recruits had presumably been educated at secondary modern
schools and had left at fourteen or fifteen years of age. The 1944
Education Act had guaranteed them a minimum secondary education,
but at the bottom end of a selective elitist system and for a shorter
time than now. Whether they had been taught to read and write by
'phonics' or by the 'look-and-say' method or in any other way seems,
sadly, to have been beside the point for these young men. There can
be little doubt that general standards of literacy were lower in 1945–
60 than they are now.

There are other general indications that standards of literacy in
Britain are likely to have risen since the Second World War. In 1950
there were fewer than twenty universities in Britain, with much smaller
student bodies than now, and since then the pendulum has swung
away from selective, elitist access to tertiary education towards a mass
tertiary education system open to all who can benefit from it. There
is also more public accountability within the system, so that its defects
are more open to scrutiny. More than 30 per cent of the relevant
age-group is now in tertiary education. It is unlikely that all of these
are literary wizards, but it is equally unlikely that any of them can be
called illiterate. What has happened is that the modern world requires
a much higher level of functional literacy from a greater proportion
of the population than in the past. We are expected to meet higher
standards. It does not of course follow that everyone will be certain
of the spellings of *supersede* and *dilapidate*: even the most highly
literate have trouble with the spelling of some such words, simply
because our orthography is complicated. We cannot measure 'literacy'

by singling out such examples (although this is what the complainers normally do).

Much of the journalistic commentary on this important question has been extremely biased and usually driven by a desire to return to traditional methods of rote learning in schools. It has been full of oversimplification and, at times, ignorance. In general, the problem (if such it is) has been presented in political terms, and those who do not exclusively advocate phonics and rote learning of 'difficult' spellings are presented as left-wing trendies (or, in the USA, 'liberals'). The imagery is that of a battlefield in which the forces of good and evil fight for the souls of our children. In the *Observer* (8 September 1996), Melanie Phillips presents the question in these terms, advocating rote learning and using headings such as 'Revenge of the Trendy Teachers'. These 'trendies' turn out to be a group of 576 university teachers of English (this must be a wide cross-section), and the letter she quotes from them is entirely reasonable. But she does not spare us the information that it was drafted by a 'Marxist', even though there is nothing Marxist in the reasoning of the letter. So we know what we are supposed to think of the letter before we read it. We can dismiss the opinion of 576 teachers of English and accept the opinion of one highly opinionated journalist, who gives no reliable evidence for her views. As for left- and right-wing politics – the British left-wing journal the *New Statesman* has often been outspoken in its defence of linguistic correctness, and one of the best-known advocates of 'liberalism' in language use is reported to have been a supporter of Mussolini. It is unhelpful to treat a serious question of this kind as if it were a political football. Teaching methods should certainly be debated, but there is no reason to believe that exclusive reliance on classroom drills and rote learning was particularly successful in the past. There was no Golden Age.

Clearly, if it were true that only systematic drills and tests would be effective in the teaching of literacy, we would have no excuse for not basing our teaching on them. But it does not seem to be true. My own experience is relevant, I think. I attended primary school in the 1940s in a rural area of Scotland. The headmistress believed in the good old methods. Almost every day we had a spelling test (having been given twenty spellings to learn). When the tests were marked, the teacher drew a chalk line on the floor and invited those who had twenty correct spellings to come forward. Those who got one wrong and two wrong were also invited to stand on chalk lines. When it got to three wrong, however, she would loudly announce 'And now the failures!' A large group of sheepish children would come forward, and the teacher would then strap them on the hand – one by one – with perhaps two or three blows for the worst spellers. It was virtually always the same children who got the strap, and there is no reason to believe that these 'good old methods' were effective at all, except to punish and demoralize dyslexics and slow learners. They never improved. This may be an extreme example, but we should bear in mind that the advocates of maximum reliance on these methods never give any evidence that they really work and never advocate safeguards to prevent maltreatment and discrimination.

If there is no evidence for declining standards of literacy, what are we to say of children's speech? This is a more complicated question, beset with even more misunderstanding than the question of literacy. The first point that must be understood is that, whereas children normally learn to read and write at school, they do not learn to speak at school. The idea that schools are responsible for teaching the basics of spoken English is therefore a myth. Spoken language is acquired without explicit instruction, and by the time the child goes to school, the basic grammar and pronunciation of the variety of language that the child is exposed to has been largely acquired. The complaints about declining standards of speaking are not normally about the child's ability to 'speak English' (although they are often phrased in this way), but about the *variety* of English that he or she speaks. Like complaints about declining literacy, they are largely untrue.

What is at issue is not the child's competence in speaking English, but his/her competence in speaking a variety known as 'standard English'. This is equated in the public mind with 'correct' English. There are two points that must be made about this variety. First, it is not well defined as a spoken variety (it is essentially a written variety), and judgements about correctness in speech are therefore often made on the basis of what is correct in writing. The 'rules' of speech are, however, very different from the 'rules' of writing. Second, in so far as it *can* be described as a spoken variety, standard speech is essentially the speech of the upper and upper-middle classes – a minority of the population. There is a very strong social dimension, and 'non-standard' accents and dialects are openly discriminated against and 'corrected', even though most people in Britain speak partly non-standard varieties. Generally, these varieties are said to be 'ungrammatical'. However, the acceptability or otherwise of these varieties is a purely social matter and has nothing to do with grammar.

Recently it has been announced that the government is to introduce 'grammar' tests for fourteen-year-olds. Among the grammatical 'errors' listed in an article in the *Independent* (19 June 1996) are the following: 'She come to my house'; 'We was going to the shops'; 'I threw it out the window'; 'The government think they can do what they like.' Of these, the last one is actually standard British English, which allows a choice between singular and plural verbs for certain collective nouns (such as *government*), but to get things wrong in this way is typical of the general incompetence of language prescriptivists. The others are widespread in spoken British English and are grammatical in non-standard varieties. Their acceptability, as we have noted, is a social matter. If they were common usage of the upper-middle classes (as *we was* used to be), they would be called 'grammatical'. It is probable, however, that the immediate reason for including sentences of this kind in 'grammar' tests is that they are not acceptable in *writing* today, even though many of them were acceptable to Shakespeare.

However, it is also proposed to teach children how to *speak* standard English in the belief that this will be good for them – it will give them more chances in life. If this is to be done by administering 'grammar' tests of the kind that seem to be contemplated, it will not work. There is in British English today a discernible tendency to level out regional differences in speech, and this process will continue regardless of grammar tests in schools. The latter in fact will merely continue the process of discriminating against non-standard speakers. In an age when discrimination in terms of race, colour, religion or gender is not publicly acceptable, the last bastion of overt social discrimination will continue to be a person's use of language.

Source

Carlo M. Cipolla, *Literacy and Development in the West* (Harmondsworth: Penguin, 1969).

In the Appalachians They Speak
like Shakespeare

Michael Montgomery

Every day thousands of motorists entering North Carolina stop at a highway welcome center for directions, refreshment or a break from the road. Until not long ago, while there they could also pick up a brief, complimentary booklet titled *A Dictionary of the Queen's English*, which was produced by the state's travel and tourism division in the mid 1960s. Its preface reads as follows:

To outsiders it sounds strange, even uncultured. But what many North Carolinians do to the King's English was done centuries ago by the Queen.

The correspondence and writings of Queen Elizabeth I and such men as Sir Walter Ralegh, Marlowe, Dryden, Bacon and even Shakespeare are sprinkled with words and expressions which today are commonplace in remote regions of North Carolina.

You hear the Queen's English in the coves and hollows of the Blue Ridge and the Great Smoky Mountains and on the windswept Outer Banks where time moves more leisurely. (c1965: 2–3)

Even for Americans unacquainted with this small publication, its existence comes as anything but a surprise. The idea that in isolated places somewhere in the country people still use 'Elizabethan' or 'Shakespearean' speech is widely held, and it is probably one of the hardier cultural beliefs or myths in the collective American psyche. Yet it lacks a definitive version and is often expressed in vague geographical and chronological terms. Since its beginning in the late nineteenth century the idea has most often been associated with the southern mountains – the Appalachians of North Carolina, Tennessee,

Kentucky and West Virginia, and the Ozarks of Arkansas and Missouri. At one extreme it reflects nothing less than a relatively young nation's desire for an account of its origins, while at the other extreme the incidental fact that English colonization of North America began during the reign of Queen Elizabeth I four centuries ago. Two things in particular account for its continued vitality: its romanticism and its political usefulness. Its linguistic validity is another matter. Linguists haven't substantiated it, nor have they tried, since the claim of Elizabethan English is based on such little evidence. But this is a secondary, if not irrelevant, consideration for those who have articulated it in print – popular writers and the occasional academic – for over a century. It has indisputably achieved the status of a myth in the sense of a powerful cultural belief.

Growing up in east Tennessee, this writer heard it said occasionally that people in the nearby mountains still spoke Elizabethan English (the location of the community was never specified), but if anything he has met the idea more often since leaving Tennessee twenty years ago. When people learn that he is a linguist who grew up near the mountains, they frequently ask, 'Isn't there supposed to be some place up there where they still speak Elizabethan English?' When asked, none could recall where they heard the idea or where the community was supposed to be. That people somewhere used Elizabethan speech was something that 'everybody just knows.'

In the United States it often forms part of a general characterization of the southern mountains as an idyllic, if rugged, locale where people have somehow been lost in time. Balladry, story-telling, traditional dancing and weaving are cited as archaic cultural features similarly preserved by people who have been isolated geographically and socially. An especially dreamy version of this appears in a 1929 article titled 'Elizabethan America' by Charles Morrow Wilson.

We know a land of Elizabethan ways – a country of Spenserian speech, Shakespearean people, and of cavaliers and curtsies. It is a land of high hopes and mystic allegiances, where one may stroll through the forests of Arden and find heaths and habits like those of olden England.

We are speaking of the Southern highlands – Appalachia and

Ozarkadia . . . Husbandmen and ploughmen in Shakespeare's England and present-day upland farmers could very likely have rubbed shoulders and swapped yarns with few misunderstandings, linguistic or otherwise; for Elizabethan English, as well as Elizabethan England, appears to have survived magnificently in these isolated Southern uplands.

The speech of the Southern mountains is a survival of the language of older days, rather than a degradation of the United States English . . . a surprisingly large number of old words have survived, along with a surprisingly large number of old ways, giving a quaint and delightful flavor of olden England. Illustrations are plentiful enough. The most casual of listeners will become conscious of the preponderance of strong preterites in mountain speech: clum *for 'climbed',* drug *for 'dragged',* wropped *for 'wrapped',* fotch *for 'fetched', and* holp *for 'helped' – all sound Elizabethanisms to be found in Shakespeare, Lovelace or the King James Bible. The Southern uplander says* fur *(for) with Sir Philip Sidney,* furder *with Lord Bacon, and in common with Hakluyt,* allow *for 'suppose'. Like Chaucer, he forms the plurals of monosyllables ending in* -st *by adding* -es: postes, beastes, jystes *(joists),* nestes *and* ghostes. *Shakespearean-like, he probably calls a salad a* sallet, *a bag a* poke *and uses* antic *for 'careful' and* bobble *for 'mix-up' . . . (1929:238–39)*

Wilson begins with such a far-fetched description that it's tempting not to take it seriously, but this passage is typical of many others. As with the miniature North Carolina dictionary cited earlier, Wilson cites writers and sources other than Shakespeare (especially Chaucer and the authorized version of the Bible). Though dating from very different centuries, these are alike in being highly prestigious texts, universally esteemed for their use of language. The 'Elizabethan English' cited is not the colorful language of Shakespeare and his contemporaries but rather common, down-to-earth verb forms like *clum* and *fotch*, which today would be considered rustic and uneducated, if not improper and illiterate. Wilson's list of words is longer than most others, but it's typical in being mainly verb past tenses, old-fashioned plurals and vocabulary that would probably not strike many as especially 'Shakespearean'.

It's not clear exactly when the idea of Shakespearean English in the mountains was first articulated, but William Goodell Frost, President of Berea College in the east Kentucky mountains, was undoubtedly most influential in promoting and establishing the view that mountain speech and culture were legitimate survivals from older times. His 1899 essay, 'Our Contemporary Ancestors', was the published form of an address given for years to alumni and contributors to his college. In it he stated:

The rude language of the mountains is far less a degradation than a survival. The [Old English] pronoun 'hit' holds its place almost universally. Strong past tenses, 'holp' for helped, 'drug' for dragged, and the like, are heard constantly; and the syllabic plural is retained in words ending in -st and others. The greeting as we ride up to a cabin is 'Howdy, strangers. 'Light and hitch your beastes.' Quite a vocabulary of Chaucer's words, which have been dropped by polite lips but which linger in these solitudes, has been made out by some of our students. 'Pack' for carry, 'gorm' for muss, 'feisty' for full of life, impertinent, are examples.

As the country experienced immigration from southern and eastern Europe in the late nineteenth century and its people became increasingly diverse, Frost and other writers focused attention on the fellow citizens of 'pure Anglo-Saxon' heritage who had yet to join the advance of American civilization. However, it was, they claimed, a misconception to view mountain people as neglected or deprived, because they had preserved much of the language and culture of the British Isles which the dominant, mainstream culture neither recognized nor valued, even though most of its own ancestors had spoken in like manner.

The Shakespearean English idea was formulated and promoted by people born and bred outside the mountains, first by educators and clergymen (Frost was both) and later by journalists and travel writers. Often these were individuals who, having come to know mountain people firsthand, wished to identify their positive qualities to a wider audience, to combat the distorted, negative images of mountain people popularized in the press. In the late nineteenth century, newspapers ran sensational stories about mountain feuding and moonshining, just as today they periodically feature accounts of snake-handling religion, high homicide rates and endemic social deprivation. Modern-day Hollywood movies like *Deliverance* have done nothing to counter this image problem. Entering the mountains with such negative stereotypes, outsiders are surprised when they 'discover' the 'true' nature of mountain speech and write as if this were a revelation. Just three years ago the Lexington (KY) *Press-Herald* ran an article by a Midwestern schoolteacher who had taken a job in a tiny, eastern Kentucky community and found that his pupils to his amazement used many 'Shakespearean' and 'Chaucerian' expressions.

For these counter-propagandists, as we might call them, identifying the Elizabethan nature of mountain speech can be accomplished by citing a mere handful of words. The issue was one of perceptions and public relations, not of linguistics.

However, the contention that mountaineers talk like Shakespeare cannot withstand even a little objective scrutiny. Here are some reasons why:

First, relatively little evidence is cited in such accounts. Supporting examples are few and highly selective – often only half a dozen are used to make far-fetched assertions about mountain language as a whole. Words are often labeled as being 'Shakespearean' or 'Chaucerian' without an accompanying citation from those authors. Some are not traceable to the sixteenth century (for instance, the *Dictionary of Queen's English* cites *tee-toncey* 'tiny', in 'I'll have just a tee-toncey piece of pie' as Elizabethan).

Second, the evidence is not persuasive. Although they may not be known to the educated, middle-class, city-dwelling outsiders who write about Shakespearean English, the terms cited can usually be found in many parts of North America and the British Isles. Here are three examples, the third of which is especially common: *afeard* 'afraid' (*A Midsummer Night's Dream* III.i.25: 'Will not the ladies be *afeard* of the lion?'); *holp* (*Richard III* I.ii.107: 'Let him thank me that *holp* to send him thither.'); and *learn* 'teach' (*Romeo and Juliet* III.ii.12: 'Learn me how to lose a winning match.')

Such shortcomings in using evidence do not restrain advocates of the

Shakespearean idea, which is not empirically based or systematically induced from facts.

Third, these accounts mix facts and images, places and times, even immigrant groups from very different parts of the British Isles. For instance, the English are sometimes lumped together with the Scotch-Irish (also called the Ulster Scots), something which amateur historians and genealogists would not do, as in the following passage, again from Charles Morrow Wilson:

Broadly speaking, the Southern highlanders are an Old England folk, English and Scotch-Irish, whose forebears came forth from Elizabethan England, a nation of young life which had just found its prime, a nation of energy and daring, a nation leaping from childhood into manhood. And the spirit of Elizabethan England has long survived the weathering of time. The first settlers brought with them Elizabethan ways of living, and these ways have lasted in a country of magnificent isolation, one little touched by the ways of a modern world.

'Elizabethan' is not used in the sense of 'the literary world of southern England in the latter half of the sixteenth century' or even 'England during the Renaissance'. Not only are immigrants from Ireland sometimes subsumed with those from England, but Chaucer (who flourished in the late fourteenth century), Dryden (in the late seventeenth) and writers from other periods are regularly cited as having used terms now employed by mountaineers. What the wide-ranging texts from which citations are drawn have in common is that they are familiar – and prestigious – canonical sources which used to be required reading in the schoolroom. (Thus they reveal more about the reading of promoters of the Shakespearean idea than about mountain speakers.)

Shakespeare and Elizabeth I lived 400 years ago, but the southern mountains have been populated by Europeans for only half that length of time. The settlers who came to North America during Elizabeth I's reign either did not survive or did not stay (the first permanent colony, Jamestown, was founded under James I). Since no one came directly from Britain to the Appalachians, we wonder how they preserved their English during the intervening period. The more one reads, the less concrete meaning 'Elizabethan' and 'Shakespearean' have. In the popular mind they appear to mean nothing more than 'old-fashioned'.

Fourth, writers make other sweeping and improbable statements, such as that mountain children have a natural affinity for Shakespeare:

It is said that when the mountaineer begins to read all, he displays so marked a preference for Shakespeare that it is invariably the works of that poet that have most frequently to be rebound in any library to which he has access. The reason he himself gives for this predilection is that the things Shakespeare makes his characters do always seem so 'natural'.
(William Aspenwall Bradley, In Shakespeare's America, *1915:436)*

More recently a flatlander who took a job as a schoolteacher in the North Carolina mountains became convinced of the Elizabethan English idea and gave his first-grade pupils Shakespeare to read, with predictably dismal results, and a scholar writing a book on producing Shakespeare in North Carolina found that theater directors and critics believed that Shakespearean language was most intelligible in the western part of the state because it was closer to the everyday speech there (Champion, 1983).

Fifth, writers routinely characterize large areas of the mountains as homogeneous, as though there were no regional and social differences. Though Elizabethan speech came to Appalachia indirectly, if it came at all, this has not prevented commentators from often labeling it 'pure'. In North Carolina, according to one writer, mountaineers use a variety of English that has forms reminiscent of Shakespeare and Chaucer and is 'purely "American" '. In Kentucky, according to another, 'the purest English on earth' is spoken.

Finally, the Shakespearean English idea ignores many things that linguists know to be true. All varieties of language change, even isolated ones and, contrary to popular impression, mountain culture has been far from isolated over the past two centuries. In vocabulary, mountain speech actually has far more innovations (terms not known in the old country) than hold-overs from the British Isles. The Shakespeare myth reflects simplistic, popular views about the static nature of traditional folk cultures, especially those in out-of-the-way places.

With so many inconsistencies and problems, no wonder that American scholars have little interest in assessing how 'Elizabethan' Appalachian speech is. Scholars would say that mountain speech has more archaisms than other types of American English, but that's about it. They certainly wouldn't put a label like 'Elizabethan' on it. But believers have no logical difficulty generalizing from a handful of words to a blanket label. Especially for them the idea of Shakespearean English has become a myth, actually a combination of two myths, an origin myth claiming to explain where mountain culture came from and a myth of the noble savage which satisfies our nostalgia for a simpler, purer past, which may never have existed but which we nevertheless long for because of the complexities and ambiguities of modern life. All of this helps innumerable Americans who have no direct experience of the mountains and who consider themselves thoroughly rational people to believe that Elizabethan English is spoken there.

The idea that somewhere in the mountains people preserve a type of speech from the days of Shakespeare is more than just a romanticization of mountain life by outsiders. Many natives believe it too, associating it with the mountains in general or at least with older, less educated people. Most likely they have picked it up from schoolteachers, and sometimes they turn it to their advantage. If you ask Charles Bradley, mayor of Gatlinburg, Tennessee, in the late nineties the self-styled 'Captain of the Smoky Mountains', what distinguishes mountain people, he'll tell you immediately that they've hung on to Elizabethan English. For insiders, the Shakespearean English idea fills a variety of purposes: foremost, affirmation that their culture has respectable, even reputable roots, but also the promotion of tourism, a college (William Goodell Frost) or even a political career. In his autobiography, *The Mountains Within Me*, Zell Miller, Governor of Georgia in the late nineties, actually names the community he describes and claims that he himself talks like Shakespeare:

If Shakespeare could have been reincarnated in Nineteenth Century

Choestoe [GA], he would have felt right at home. The open fireplaces, spinning wheels, handmade looms, Greek lamps and good, if sometimes ungrammatical, Elizabethan English would all have been quite familiar to the Bard of Avon and, with the exception of having to adapt to homespun clothes, he would have had little difficulty assimilating into mountain society ... It no longer bothers me to be kidded about my mountain expressions. In fact, I have come to regard them as status symbols because who else do we have running around in public life today who speaks the language of Chaucer and Shakespeare as distilled, literally and figuratively, by two centuries of Georgia Mountain usage?

For mountain people the idea appears to be as prevalent as ever.

The Shakespearean English idea argues that isolation and the lack of modern education have caused words and meanings to survive in the mountains identical to ones used in the Elizabethan period, often considered the liveliest and richest flowering of literature in the language. These have either disappeared from mainstream/dominant culture or become labeled as illiterate or vulgar by it. Because their ancestry is forgotten or misunderstood, their modern-day speakers are wrongly labeled. At the same time, mainstream culture has lost its awareness of its own roots, those who espouse the Shakespeare idea seem to be saying.

Being a cultural repository has helped regions like Appalachia and the Ozarks define themselves against mainstream cultures that possess immense socio-economic power and prominence. Though lacking a cultural memory and having no conscious roots of its own other than a few two-dimensional, textbook images, mass American culture has created an ideology that dominates regional and ethnic cultures and articulates and imparts a value system through the media, the educational system and a variety of institutions. Less well endowed economically and absent from the pages of the nation's history, regional cultures find themselves marginalized by modern nation states, centralized institutions and educational establishments. Consequently, their speech is viewed by those in power as rustic, if not backward and uncouth. As much as anything else, it is this lack of status (both in North America and the British Isles – where it is most commonly associated with Ireland) that has led people to elaborate and advocate the 'Shakespearean myth' to bring status and recognition to these cultures.

This explains perhaps why for Appalachia there have been so many expositions of the same idea decade after decade. Advancing the idea, improbable as it is, that mountain people speak like Shakespeare counters the prevailing ideology of the classroom and society at large that unfairly handicaps rural mountain people as uneducated and unpolished and that considers their language to be a corruption of proper English. This modern ideology not only forms the backdrop against which the Shakespearean myth is articulated, but ironically it turns the history of the language on its head by dismissing its 'ancient legitimate lineage', as one writer called it not long ago (Hays 1975).

One of the most interesting aspects of the subject is the contrast between images, at least in Appalachia. Even today the name of the region conjures up images of poor diets, proneness to violence and countless other chronic ills, and social psychologists into the present generation have labored to examine the region in terms of deprivation theory. There is an obvious tension between heavily romanticized images and the jarringly negative ones, each being a product of selection of features.

Without a cultural memory, mainstream culture has little perspective to understand the true origin of mountain culture, whether this is Elizabethan or anything else, and it sometimes makes for profound misapprehensions. This calls for cultural education, which should begin locally but which at some point will probably run counter to mainstream society because it is the latter which usually chooses what is to be valued and what is not. The regional or ethnic culture has little, if any, role in the evaluation of itself. The evaluation made by mass society often produces a schizophrenia, especially among upwardly mobile members of a regional or minority culture, as they are asked to choose between two value systems and ways of talking. Mountain people may talk like Shakespeare, but in the schoolroom nothing should be permitted but 'standard English'.

At the beginning of this essay the idea of Shakespearean English being spoken today, on the eve of the third millennium, probably appeared to be something between nostalgia and a fable. But it has been a very persistent idea, and commentators a century ago did identify the crux of the matter – that natives of the mountains deserve respect as culture bearers – even though they did not contextualize it in terms of a socio-economic dynamic. They recognized some of its educational implications, however questionable its validity was in reality. Today Americans have almost no awareness of the roots of their English, and whatever respect they may have for regional cultures often does not extend to regional speech. All this means that there's definitely a place for the Shakespearean myth as an educational and political tool for the foreseeable future. Since it reflects only a small portion of reality, it would be wise for linguists to play a role in working out its pedagogical applications, but even they must appreciate that it has achieved the status of a myth.

Some Languages Have No Grammar
Winifred Bauer

It is not uncommon to hear people say (usually derogatorily) of a language 'It doesn't have any grammar.' To appreciate the absurdity of this statement, it is helpful to specify what 'grammar' is. For linguists, the 'grammar' of a language is the set of rules which the speakers of the language follow when they speak. It encompasses rules about the possible forms of words (*shplernk* is not a possible word in English), rules about the way bits of words can be put together (you can't make plurals in English by putting the *-s* first), rules about the way words are put together to make longer units (in English you have to say *This is an interesting book*, not *A book interesting is this*) and rules about the way meanings are encoded by speakers. For some non-linguists, 'grammar' refers only to the second and third of these types of rules. Even on that narrower definition, it is easy to demonstrate that all languages have grammar.

For argument's sake, let us discuss the proposition 'Spelitzian has no grammar.' I shall demonstrate that this cannot be true by considering what Spelitzian would be like if it were true.

If Spelitzian had no grammar, it would be impossible to make a mistake when speaking Spelitzian. Saying that a sentence is wrong in Spelitzian is the same as saying that it breaks a rule or rules of Spelitzian. If Spelitzian has rules, then it has grammar.

If Spelitzian had no grammar, there could be no difference between nouns and verbs or other word classes. There could be no pronouns, because they – by definition – stand for nouns, not verbs, and thus imply a distinction between the classes. If it is possible to distinguish word classes in Spelitzian, Spelitzian has grammar. All known human languages distinguish at least nouns and verbs.

...zian had no grammar, there could be no rules for the ...t of words in sentences. Every order would be possible in ...ase. To say 'John said Pip hit the fence,' you could say the e... valent of 'Pip say john hit fence,' 'Fence say john hit pip,' 'Hit say fence pip john,' 'Say fence john pip hit,' or any other of the 120 possible word orders! Each of these would, of course, also be able to mean 'Pip said John hit the fence,' and other things like 'John, say "The fence hit Pip."' Clearly, the listener would not know what was intended. Such a 'language' would only allow people to communicate extremely simple messages, probably only one-word messages.

If Spelitzian had no grammar, it could not have prefixes or suffixes, for example. These would imply that Spelitzian had rules for forming words, and thus that it had grammar. (If English had no rules for the placement of such forms, then *pots* could equally well be replaced by *spot*, *psot* or *post* on any occasion. Imagine what would happen if you tried to say 'Spot the pots on the post.')

If Spelitzian had no grammar, it could not have 'little words' (particles) to mark grammatical functions. Suppose it had a conjunction like *and*. If it could not be fixed in position, you would not know what it joined, so it would be possible to say 'Pip and Pat like John' by the Spelitzian equivalent for 'pip and john like pat' or 'pat pip john and like.' Particles work because they occur in specified positions in relation to other words.

If Spelitzian had no grammar, it would not be possible to mark the differences between sentences by changing the 'tune' or intonation of the sentence. Thus it would not be possible to mark differences between statements, questions and commands, between *Pip hit Pat*, *Pip hit Pat?* (or *Did Pip hit Pat?*) and *Pip, hit Pat*. If Spelitzian used intonation to mark these changes, the intonation would have a grammatical function, and thus Spelitzian would have grammar. In all known human languages these differences are conveyed by some combination of word order, modification of word forms (e.g. adding a suffix), function-marking particles and intonation.

To sum up, if Spelitzian distinguishes different word classes it has grammar. If Spelitzian has rules about word order, it has grammar. If Spelitzian has rules about the addition of prefixes, suffixes, etc., it has grammar. If Spelitzian has particles which 'go with' particular types of words (such as prepositions like *to*, *in*, *by*), it has grammar. If Spelitzian uses different 'tunes' which change the meaning of what the speaker of Spelitzian says, it has grammar.

If Spelitzian had none of these, then when two speakers of this 'language' were talking, the listener would not know what the speaker intended. At best the listener would guess. With such an imprecise system, language would be of very little use. Such a system resembles what we know of very simple animal communication systems. No human languages we know behave like this. All allow the precise communication of complex messages, and this requires grammar.

Next I will consider whether it is true that some languages don't have very much grammar, or that some languages have more grammar than others. Latin is often taken by non-linguists as the 'standard' against which other languages are measured. Is it possible for Spelitzian to have less grammar than Latin?

There are several classes of nouns in Latin, and each class has a special pattern of endings, different in singular and plural, which mark the functions of nouns in sentences. I will illustrate with the first two classes (or declensions, as they are usually called). *Puella* 'girl' is 1st declension (feminine), and *dominus*, 'lord' is 2nd declension (masculine):

1st Declension	*Singular*	*Plural*
Nominative	puell-a	puell-ae
Vocative	puell-a	puell-ae
Accusative	puell-am	puell-ās
Genitive	puell-ae	puell-ārum
Dative	puell-ae	puell-īs
Ablative	puell-ā	puell-īs

2nd Declension	*Singular*	*Plural*
Nominative	domin-us	domin-ī
Vocative	domin-e	domin-ī
Accusative	domin-um	domin-ōs

Genitive	domin-ī	domin-ōrum
Dative	domin-ō	domin-īs
Ablative	domin-ō	domin-īs

In basic terms, the nominative is used for the subject of a sentence (the person or thing that performs the action), the vocative is used to mark the person or thing addressed, the accusative is used for the direct object of a sentence (the person or thing which is affected by the action), the genitive is used for possessors of things, the dative is used for the goal of an action (*to* phrases) and the ablative is used for *by, with* and *from* phrases. Thus to say 'The girl saw the lord' in Latin, *girl* is translated with the form *puella*, the nominative, and *lord* is translated with *dominum*, the accusative. To say 'O girls, bow to your lord!', *girls* would be translated with the vocative plural form *puellae*, *lord* would be translated with the dative singular *domino*, and *your* would require the genitive form of the pronoun.

Latin verbs also have patterns of endings which mark person, number and tenses, as in the following list of endings for one type of verb (first conjugation) in present and perfect tenses:

	Present		*Perfect*	
	Singular	*Plural*	*Singular*	*Plural*
1st (I, we)	am-ō	amā-mus	amā-vī	amā-vimus
2nd (you)	amā-s	amā-tis	amā-vistī	amā-vistis
3rd (he/she)	ama-t	ama-nt	amā-vit	amā-vērunt

Because Latin words carry on their ends markers which show their function, Latin has relatively free word order. Thus 'The girl saw the lord' can be translated by any of the following: *Puella vidit dominum, Vidit puella dominum, Dominum vidit puella, Puella dominum vidit, Vidit dominum puella, Dominum puella vidit.* All possible orders are in theory acceptable, although some are much more usual than others. (However, it should be noted that Latin word order is not entirely free: such forms as conjunctions and some adverbs have specific places in relation to the sentence as a whole or to other word classes.)

The way Latin works has led to the perception that 'grammar' means sets of endings. The fact that Latin also has rules for word order is often ignored. You cannot jumble completely freely the words in the Latin sentence equivalent to 'John said the girl saw the lord,' although there are several possible orders.

Many languages do not have sets of endings on nouns and verbs like Latin. Modern English has very few in comparison with Latin (and in comparison with Old English). Chinese has none at all. However, we cannot conclude that English has less grammar than Latin and Chinese none at all. English has replaced a Latin-like system of endings on nouns and free word order with a system of few endings and fixed word order. The fixed word order has the effect of marking the function of words just as clearly as the use of endings. Consider (a) *The girl protected the lord* and (b) *The lord protected the girl*. The performer of the action always comes before the verb *protected*, and the recipient of the action always comes after the verb. In (a) we know that the girl performed the action with just as much certainty as in the equivalent Latin sentence. Thus fixed word order in English does the same job as the marking of nominative and accusative on nouns in Latin. Chinese also uses word order to mark these functions.

Yet other languages use particles to mark these functions. Maori has a particle *i*, which occurs before the recipient of the action and contrasts with no particle before the performer of the action. Thus in Maori 'the girl' is *te kōtiro*, *te ariki* is 'the lord' and 'protected' is *ka tiaki*, so *Ka tiaki te kōtiro i te ariki* is 'The girl protected the lord' and *Ka tiaki te ariki i te kōtiro* is 'The lord protected the girl.' While it is usual for the actor to precede the recipient, as in these sentences, it is possible under some circumstances to reverse the order, as in *Ka tiaki i te kōtiro te ariki*, which still means 'The lord protected the girl' and cannot mean 'The girl protected the lord.' Thus particles are another grammatical device parallel to endings and word order for marking such grammatical functions.

Since all three means are equivalent, a language which uses word order or particles has a grammatical system equivalent to one which uses endings. Latin, which makes extensive use of endings (or inflections), Chinese, which uses word order, Maori, which uses particles and relatively fixed word order, and English, which uses fixed word order and some inflections all have equivalent grammatical systems in this regard. Once we accept that languages can make similar distinctions using different sorts of grammatical devices, it becomes clear that it is very difficult to quantify how much 'grammar' a language has, and thus statements like 'Spelitzian has hardly any grammar' or 'Latin has more grammar than Spelitzian' cannot readily be supported. You have to consider the kinds of grammatical distinctions a language makes, not how it makes them.

While all known human languages mark basic distinctions such as the differences between the actor and the recipient of an action or between statements, questions and commands, there are still many other distinctions which are marked in some languages, but not in others. It is not true that Latin (or any other language) marks all the possible grammatical distinctions, and other languages mark only a subset of them. Here I can only hint at some of the wealth of differences in what languages mark.

English marks a difference between 'definite' noun phrases and 'indefinite' noun phrases by (amongst other things) the use of *a* and *the*. Latin does not mark this distinction at all. Maori makes a distinction somewhat similar to that in English, also through articles roughly comparable to *a* and *the*, while Chinese makes a somewhat similar distinction through word order. In this field, then, Latin makes fewest grammatical distinctions.

There are American-Indian languages which distinguish between things which happened recently in the past and things which happened a long time ago, and between things which speakers know from their own experience and things which they've been told. So in these languages, I would require a different form of the verb *lose* to say in 1996 'England lost to Germany in the semi-finals' and to say in 1996 'The English lost the battle of Hastings in 1066.' And both of these (which I only know because I have been told so) would require a different verb from 'I lost my game of Scrabble this afternoon,' which I know from my own experience.

Some languages, like Maori, have different pronouns for *we* when it means 'you the listener and me the speaker' and when it means 'me the speaker and someone else, like my mother'. And Fijian, in addition, has not just singular and plural pronouns, but singular, dual (for two people), trial (for three people) and plural pronouns. European languages have relatively simple pronoun systems, although they distinguish gender in the third person, which Maori and Fijian do not.

Examples like these show that language A may have more complex systems than language B in one area and less complex systems in other areas. We cannot sensibly quantify the amount of grammar a language has. All languages have immensely complex grammatical systems.

Sometimes when people assert that a language has no grammar, what they really mean is that there is no grammar book for that particular language. But the rules of a language exist in the heads of speakers of that language. We know the rules are there because of the way the speakers behave. They use similar structures for similar events. If you hear the Spelitzian sentence for 'Give me some water,' you can be pretty sure you can use the same pattern for 'Give me some food,' even if there are other possible patterns as well. If there weren't any patterns, people wouldn't be able to communicate because they would have no way of knowing what other people meant to say. You can understand what I say only because you know the same rules I do. That is what it means to speak the same language. Speakers can tell you whether a particular string of words is an acceptable sentence of their language. You, as a speaker of English, know that 'Spelitzian isn't a real language' is a possible sentence of English, even though I feel confident that you have never met it before. And you know, equally well, that 'Spelitzian real language isn't' is not a possible sentence of English. You do not need a grammar book to tell you this. Your own internal grammar tells you.

A grammar book of a language contains rules which mirror the rules speakers use when they speak that language. You can work out the rules which must be in the heads of speakers of Spelitzian by observing what they say. Suppose the following were sentences of Spelitzian:

> *Mashak Spelitziask op Pat*
> 'The Spelitzian saw Pat.'
> *Mashak Pat op Speltiziask*
> 'Pat saw the Spelitzian.'
>
> *Trakak Spelitziask op Pat*
> 'The Spelitzian greeted Pat'
> *Trakak Pat op Spelitziask*
> 'Pat greeted the Spelitzian.'

On the basis of these sentences, we might deduce the following patterns: the verb comes first, followed by the performer, followed by the recipient. The recipient always has *op* in front of it. We could start to write a grammar book for Spelitzian by writing down these rules, although they would almost certainly need some refinement as we accounted for other sentences. Every time we noticed a new pattern which Spelitzians follow, that would tell us about a new rule of Spelitzian, and we could add it to the grammar book. That is how grammar books are written. Thus the existence of a grammar book is irrelevant to the question of whether the language has grammar. A grammar book can be written for any language, because every language has grammar.

If Spelitzian is a language, it has a highly complex grammatical system, involving some combination of devices like word order, inflections, particles and intonation. A language without any grammar is a contradiction in terms.

Italian is Beautiful, German is Ugly

Howard Giles and Nancy Niedzielski

The title of this essay reflects the commonly held view, at least among many English-speakers, that certain languages are more aesthetically pleasing than others. Italian – even for those who cannot speak the language – sounds elegant, sophisticated and lively. French is similarly viewed as romantic, cultured and sonorous. These languages conjure up positive emotions in hearers – and perhaps, generally more pleasing moods in their speakers. In contrast, German, Arabic and some East-Asian tongues accomplish the opposite: they are considered harsh, dour and unpleasant-sounding.

The English language is probably somewhere in the middle, evoking few accolades of aesthetic merit but few comments of utter disdain. It undoubtedly triggers feelings of linguistic and cultural pride when, for instance, evocative poetry in the language is being read or when national institutions (e.g. the language used on national TV news) are purportedly being threatened from outside by other language groups. Here, then, we have the first hints that judgments about a language variety's beauty are dependent on the nature of the context in which the views are being expressed and tied to the fabric of our national and social identities, which we take up later.

If we dig further, we find that different varieties of English are accorded different degrees of pleasantness. The sounds of British English are coveted in certain North American communities, and speakers of it will be constantly greeted with exclamations to the effect, 'My, your accent is so delightful . . . do speak more.' This is often followed by the caution: 'Never lose that delightful way of talking,' and in essence, therefore, talk like 'us'. In Britain, studies we have performed have shown that various accents are considered quite vulgar (e.g. Birmingham, London Cockney). Indeed, the stronger the accent, the more contempt will abound. In one famous sociolinguistic survey, a Glaswegian commented: 'It's the slovenly speech in the industrial areas that I don't care for – these industrialized cities – I don't like the accent they have.'

On the other hand, British accents from some rural areas are considered 'charming', 'lilting' and 'quaint', such as some of the South-Welsh dialects (of course there are many South Welsh accents too, such as Carmarthen, which recent studies have shown to be less folksy).

Despite another myth to the contrary, rigidly held views of accent pleasantness–unpleasantness are hardly a 'British disease'! In Australia, a broad accent is considered 'vulgar'. In France, a Parisian brogue is considered more cultivated than a French Canadian accent or the nearer-to-home Breton accent. In the USA, Appalachian, Texan, certain Southern and New York accents are an affront to the ear (at least outside those areas) whereas a New England variety is considered consensually more standard and comely. Black Vernacular English (or the more recent, controversial notion of 'Ebonics') incurs the same fate as the former varieties for many of those who are not African-American (as well as a number who are). We could continue on to Spain and most other cultures and the story would mostly be the same with their varieties.

In sum, most of us have our favorite-sounding languages and dialects. Even single sounds, such as the gutturals (e.g. the glottal stop, as in Cockney 'bottle') and nasality are disparaged. As John Honey has commented in his 1989 guide to British pronunciation, 'most people who comment on differences between standard and non-standard accents believe that the basis of their judgments is aesthetics – a matter of taste such as distinguishes a good piece of music from a bad one, a good painting from a daub, a good poem from a piece of meretricious verse.'

Why then should we have such well-defined views of language beauty and ugliness? Two competing views exist. The first has been called the 'inherent value hypothesis'. As the term implies, advocates of this position claim that some languages (and accents of them) are inherently more attractive than others. Simply put, it has nothing to do with historical preferences or social conditioning, rather, certain ways of being 'nicely spoken' are biologically wired into us. It is for this reason alone that certain language forms assume prestige over others. These others could not possibly ever gain superiority or become 'the standard' since they are too harsh, vulgar and unpleasant. Language scholars and historians in the past have held strongly to this argument. As one of them put it, 'if one were to compare every vowel sound ... in standard British English ... with the corresponding sounds in non-standard accents, no unbiased observer would hesitate to prefer ... [the former] ... as the most pleasing and sonorous form.'

Strong words indeed, but why should we – as thinking people – care about this so-called 'fact of life' or even nature? The answer is that it has woeful implications for society, three of which we shall highlight. First, too many speakers of certain languages and dialects are brought up believing, sometimes via ridicule and abuse, that their way of communicating – a fundamental aspect of their identity and who they are – is grossly inadequate. Unfortunately, then, some speakers are embarrassed about how they talk. As one informant having a Norwich (England) accent reported, 'I talk horrible.' This phenomenon has been called 'linguistic self-hatred'.

No wonder then that certain educational institutions denigrate the way certain ethnic minorities and lower-working-class children talk. Such institutions, teachers, and even parents, attempt to obliterate this expression of themselves to accommodate a 'better' way of talking. This is not meant to indicate that this approach is not well intentioned – yet we regard its underlying values as misguided.

Second, we have shown in past research that there is a strong link between the perceived pleasantness of a language variety and the apparent intelligibility of what is said in it. It is important to understand here that a person's comprehensibility is not an incontestable 'linguistic fact'. Oftentimes, our views about a dialect (and its speakers) can color our beliefs about whether we can understand it and particularly our willingness to expend effort after interpreting it. Construing a particular dialect as, say, 'vulgar' and feeling discomfort and dissatisfaction when talking to speakers of it can unwittingly bias our perceptions of its intelligibility – hence, ultimately, its worth as a viable form of communication.

Third and relatedly, how 'well' we speak can have great social currency. In the initial survey mentioned, one informant claimed that 'if you were an employer and somebody came in to see you with a broad Glaswegian accent and then another man came in with an English accent, you'd be more inclined to give the English man the job because he had a nicer way of speaking.' Likewise, research has shown, across cultures, that speaking in a way that is consensually agreed upon to be unpleasant would lead to some unfavorable social consequences. These might include when one is being diagnosed in a clinic, when giving evidence in court, seeking housing and when seeking statusful employment.

We, and most language scholars, do not embrace the inherent value hypothesis – we believe it to be a flagrant, yet understandable, social myth. Rather, we are advocates of a totally different position that, together with Peter Trudgill, we have previously labeled the 'social connotations hypothesis'. As this term implies, we favor a view proposing that the pleasantness or unpleasantness of a language variety is a time-honored social convention. The pleasantness, or otherwise, of a language variety (and hence the emotive qualities associated with it) are contingent on the social attributes of the speakers of it. Thus, if a social group (such as an ethnic elite or social class) assumes power in a society, it will take measures to have its form of communication privileged through the media, education, and so forth. Historically, this comes about in a variety of ways. First, it can be established overtly through public policy and language laws, as in the case of legislation across many American states making English the official language. Next, it can be established through strategic attempts to obliterate the non-prestige varieties – as happened with 'Spanish' languages other than Castilian in the Franco era.

Other times, it happens (arguably far less intentionally and more covertly over long time-periods) when communities begin to connote status and aesthetics with speaking in a societally valued manner. Indeed, the social origins of our views about dialects are deeply rooted. Our own developmental studies have shown that the emotional grounding for this can be laid down as early as three or four years of age! Interestingly also, we have found that while (non-standard-sounding) children of six would laugh and disparage the accents of prestige speakers, by nine years of age they had been socialized into accepting unhesitatingly just such prestige forms to emulate. Findings from Italy also echo the inclination for children to like non-standard speech until they spend time in the school system.

In terms of the social connotations hypothesis then, standard British English and French are not inherently superior and elegant forms of communication but, rather, are so largely due to the fact that the Court and other spheres of social, commercial and political influence flourished in particular geographical centers (viz. London and Paris respectively). Had they been established in other areas, these very same so-called standard varieties would have been relatively trivialized, perhaps suffering the same fate as other urban dialects like Glaswegian.

We find, then, that if you were to survey British people and ask them to rate how pleasant it would be to live in various cities and regions and then ask them to rate the pleasantness of the accents of these locales, there would be a very high correlation indeed between these two assessments. Studies have even shown that speakers of prestige language forms are judged more handsome and physically attractive!

In sum, it is the social connotations of the speakers of a language variety – whether they are associated with poverty, crime and being uneducated on the one hand, or cultured, wealthy and having political muscle on the other – that dictates our aesthetic (and other) judgments about the language variety. This is not an uncomplicated equation, of course, and language 'facts' can sometimes swiftly change – a process that supports this argument. To illustrate, we offer the 'Black is beautiful' or 'Welsh is beautiful' (among many other) movements. When subordinate groups in society come to question the legitimacy of their inferior roles in society and attribute these to oppressive and discriminatory measures of an 'elite' group, they can redefine the beauty and importance of their language, accordingly, and sometimes vociferously. Whether the dominant group will readily accede to such demands and allied actions and thereby allow their own language varieties to necessarily lose some of their aesthetic sway, is another interesting phenomenon that falls somewhat under the purview of the social psychology of intergroup relations. This is part of the process of how languages and dialects change, die and are even resurrected.

This is not to say that although there is a strong correspondence between the perceived status of a variety and its aesthetic value, it is a one-to-one relationship. In one study in the 1970s we found that while the German accent in British English was rated as having higher status than any regional accents of Britain studied therein, its rated pleasantness was much lower. Here again, however, the social connotations hypothesis holds its own. Britons had mixed feelings in this case. On the one hand, the accent was associated by many with certain members of that nation's desires for world domination and the atrocities and hardships that attended that move. On the other it was conceded that this group now (ironically also for some) had achieved immense prosperity and economic influence. Arguably, aesthetic judgments prevailed with the former image while status judgments inclined after the latter. In addition, work in the context of the 'gender-linked language effect' has shown over a host of studies that while the speech and writing of males is upgraded in terms of competence and dynamism, it is downgraded in terms of aesthetics.

What other insights, as well as research, inform our belief that the title of this essay constitutes a myth? We and others have found that judgments of linguistic beauty are determined in large part by the larger context in which they are embedded. That is, linguistic aesthetics do not come in a social vacuum and few, if any, inherent values exist. This can be illustrated in a number of ways. First, who is speaking the language variety (e.g. an attractive member of the opposite sex or a member of one's own ingroup) and who is doing the judging can be critical to outcomes. It may come as little surprise to know that when asking Israelis whether Arabic or Hebrew is more pleasing, musical or rich, for instance, Jews rate the latter, while Arabs rate the former as higher, both rating their own ingroup tongue preferentially.

In addition, imagine rating the pleasantness of the same (neutral) Italian message under three very different circumstances: (a) enjoying gourmet Tuscan food and wine whilst being serenaded by a delightful Verdi aria; (b) doing this 'cold' under survey conditions; and (c) reading a newspaper account of a supposed Mafia atrocity. Pleasantness ratings under (a) conditions would be elevated over those in (b) and might even veer towards unpleasantness in the social climate of (c). Correspondingly, the 'ugliness' of German might dissipate rapidly when listening to an engaging Mozart opera whilst partaking of delicious Swiss-German Emmental cheese or delicate Austrian tortes washed down with either a first-rate Beerenausler wine or a remarkable Bavarian beer.

Research thus shows that sounds are in the ear of the beholder, to be variably interpreted and socially constructed, rather than 'out there' as some fact to be objectively measured. As a final example, if an American associates Spanish or Asian languages with a 'cultural invasion', a threat to jobs, national or linguistic integrity, he or she is much more likely to consider them ugly languages than if the languages are associated with long-standing civilizations, art or fashion. More personally and anecdotally, we have known people who have had rigid views about the ugliness of Irish and Australian accents, undoubtedly due to the profoundly negative stereotypes (e.g. brash, uncultured) associated with speakers of these varieties. However, when visiting these countries and finding the people unexpectedly and extremely hospitable, generous, fun and quick-witted, not only did their views shift dramatically in favor of the delight of the accents, but they were even accommodated in our friends' speech!

Finally, together with Richard Bourhis, Peter Trudgill and colleagues, we have in a series of studies investigated the merit of the social connotations hypothesis. As a backdrop, French Canadians have traditionally favored the Parisian dialect over local forms of French in terms of elegance and pleasantness, just as the Greeks have favored the standard Athenian accent over the Cretan variety. The inherent value hypothesis would propose that English-speakers totally unfamiliar with either French or Greek would share these natural preferences. Not so. Our English judges (having, of course, no social connotations associated with these sounds) rated the corresponding standard and non-standard varieties equally favorably.

In another study, we asked American and Canadian listeners to rate a variety of British regionally accented speakers whose ratings varied considerably in terms of pleasantness for local British judges. While they were obviously familiar with the language *per se* (unlike the previous studies), once again they did not discriminate the varieties in terms of pleasantness. For us, this was due to the fact that they had no knowledge whatsoever attending what it was socially, and stereotypically, to be a speaker of these accents; Cockney, one of the most denigrated British varieties, sounded as fine to the Americans as any other variety.

To conclude, we believe views about the beauty and ugliness of languages and dialects are built on cultural norms, pressures and social connotations. We could have spread our net, of course, far wider, to make similar arguments about other stigmatized aesthetic forms, such as the language of the elderly, homosexuals, Creoles, and so forth. Yet, and as we have argued elsewhere, we cannot tell people that their aesthetic responses are false; that would be unrealistic and counter-productive, as the Ebonics issue in the United States clearly illustrates. Rather, we should encourage teachers and others not to abandon these judgments entirely but to recognize them for what they are: the result of a complex of social, cultural, regional, political and personal associations and prejudices. Most listeners know of linguistic varieties that they do not like, but we should appreciate that these feelings are highly subjective and have no basis in social scientific fact. In particular, such feelings should not be allowed to influence teachers', the media's and politicians' attitudes and policies towards children's and others' language varieties – the more so since they are likely to breed linguistic insecurity and are, in any case, almost certainly not shared by all members of the wider culture. In the classroom, there is a huge and important difference between the 'German is ugly,' statement of apparent fact, and 'I personally find German speech unattractive,' which, even if better left unsaid, is nevertheless a recognition of the subjectivity of responses due to social connotations.

The case for us language scholars is not cut and dried. We, for our part, would wish to continue with more programmatic research to determine precisely the changing, multidimensional aspects of aesthetic preference for various modes of communication (e.g. written, and new communication technology) that are laid down when, how, where and why and with what social repercussions over time.

Sources and further reading

For more details on how people socially evaluate language varieties, see chapter 2 of Howard Giles and Nikolaus Coupland, *Language: Contexts and Consequences* (Pacific Grove, CA: Brooks/Cole, 1992); for the inherent value versus the social connotations hypotheses, including more details of the experiments outlined above, see the chapter by Peter Trudgill and Howard Giles, 'Sociolinguistics and linguistic value judgements', in *Proceedings of a Colloquium on the Functionality of Language* (Ghent: Studia Scientia, 1976).

Bad Grammar is Slovenly

Lesley Milroy

Like most language myths this one begs a number of questions, such as the following:

What is meant by 'bad grammar'?
What is meant by 'grammar'?
Can particular sentences of the English language reasonably be
   described as 'slovenly' – or 'lacking in care and precision',
   according to one dictionary definition?

The quest for answers exposes the myth to critical scrutiny.

Newspaper features, letter columns and the mailboxes of the BBC are good places to find complaints about bad grammar. A rich harvest may be gathered if language use becomes the subject of public debate or if current educational policies are focusing on English teaching and testing. In Britain recently many judgemental remarks have been aired about 'Estuary English', the name given to a variety of the language which is spreading both socially and geographically.

Examples of specific constructions often described as bad grammar can be placed in at least three categories. The first, exemplified in sentences (1)–(3) along with the (presumed) correct form in italics, regularly occur in the speech and writing of educated people.

(1) Who am I speaking to? / *To whom am I speaking?*
(2) Martha's two children are completely different to each
   other. / *Martha's two children are completely different from each
   other.*

(3) I want to quickly visit the library. / *I want to visit the library quickly.*

Two well-known 'errors' appear in (1), namely the preposition in the sentence final position and the nominative form of the relative pronoun 'who' rather than the oblique form 'whom' which is prescribed after a preposition. In (2) the expression 'different to' is used rather than the prescribed 'different from'; and in (3) there is a 'split infinitive'. In fact, the 'correct' versions were prescribed as such relatively recently in the history of the language, as part of the flurry of scholarly activity associated with the codification of the English language in the eighteenth century. Since the goal of codification is to define a particular form as standard, this process entailed intolerance of the range of choices which speakers and writers had hitherto taken for granted. In earlier centuries all these 'errors' appeared in highly sophisticated writing; in 1603, for example, Thomas Decker wrote 'How much different art thou to this cursed spirit here?'

Different rationalizations were introduced to support these new prescriptions. The model of Latin was invoked to argue that a preposition should not end a sentence, that the inflected form of *who* should not appear anywhere other than in the subject of the sentence, and that an infinitive should not be split. The reason advanced by one writer of a popular manual of correctness for preferring 'different from' is that 'different to' is illogical, since no one would say 'similar from'. But it is not difficult to construct an equally logical argument in support of 'different to', since it falls into a set of words with comparative meanings such as *similar, equal, superior*, which require *to*. Not only are prescriptive arguments difficult to sustain, but if taken seriously they are likely to create problems. For example, 'Who am I speaking to?' is normal in most contexts, while 'To whom am I speaking?' will generally be interpreted as marking social distance. Thus the real difference between these forms is stylistic; both are good English sentences in appropriate contexts. Sometimes an attempt to follow the prescribed rules produces odd results.

(4) A good author needs to develop a clear sense of who she is writing for.

(5) A good author needs to develop a clear sense of for whom she is writing.

The prescription, which outlaws (4) and yields (5), does not work because it is not based on a principled analysis of the structure of English but is a response to cultural and political pressures. By the eighteenth century Britain needed a standardized language to meet the needs of geographically scattered colonial government servants and to facilitate mass education. It did not too much matter which of a set of variants emerged as standard, as long as only one was specified as such. The prescribed standard was codified in grammars (such as Robert Lowth's) and dictionaries (the most famous being Dr Johnson's). No systematic grammar of English existed at that time, but Latin had a particular prestige as the lingua franca of scholars throughout Europe; hence the appeal not only to logic but to the model of Latin to justify particular prescriptions. But as we shall see shortly, English rules are very different from Latin rules, though equally complex; like all Germanic languages, English quite naturally places prepositions in sentence final position.

By 'bad grammar' then is sometimes meant expressions which are not in line with even unrealistic prescriptions. But what is grammar? Our myth refers to a *prescriptive* grammar, which is not a systematic description of a language, but a sort of linguistic etiquette, essentially an arbitrary set of *do*s and *don't*s. Two other kinds of grammar can be distinguished – a *descriptive* grammar and a *mental* grammar.

A descriptive grammar does not set out to legislate on correctness but describes how words are patterned to form major constituents of sentences. The distinctive rules of English which underlie these patterns are acquired by children and learnt by speakers of other languages but are generally taken for granted by prescriptive grammars. One basic rule of this type describes how questions are formed in English. Consider the following declarative sentences and their corresponding questions:

(6) Martha is Peter's sister.

(7) Martha is cooking lasagne for dinner tonight.

(8) Martha should have cooked lasagne for dinner tonight.

(9) My new flatmate who has won the Cordon Bleu cooking contest is celebrating with a party tonight.

(10) Martha cooks lasagne every Friday.

(6a) Is Martha Peter's sister?

(7a) Is Martha cooking lasagne for dinner tonight?

(8a) Should Martha have cooked lasagne for dinner tonight?

(9a) Is my new flatmate who has won the Cordon Bleu cooking contest celebrating with a party tonight?

(10a) Does Martha cook lasagne every Friday?

Sentence (6) makes the rule seem simple: the verb moves to the beginning of the sentence. However, (7) and (8) contain a complex verb phrase, consisting of a lexical verb and one or more auxiliary verbs. Lexical verbs can be identified as dictionary entries and form an almost infinitely large class which is constantly being augmented by new borrowings and inventions: examples are *kick, sneeze, vegetate, computerize, shuttle, chortle, debug* (some of these words can behave both as verbs and nouns). The set of auxiliary verbs, however, is sharply limited: it consists of forms of *be* (such as *is* and *are*); forms of *have*; forms of *do*; and modals such as *must, should, might, could, can, will*. As (7) and (8) show, the question-formation rule moves the *first* auxiliary verb to the beginning of the sentence. But (9) shows that this does not always work. Simply moving the first auxiliary verb produces a truly ungrammatical sentence which is not in line with the rules used by any speaker of any kind of English. This kind of sentence is conventionally marked with a star:

(11) *Has my new flatmate who won the Cordon Bleu cooking contest is celebrating with a party tonight?

To solve this problem we need to modify our rule; the subject of the sentence changes places with the next auxiliary verb, which ends up at the front of the sentence. The subject of (9) is shown in italics:

(12) *My flatmate who has won the Cordon Bleu cooking contest* is celebrating with a party tonight.

Subjects of sentences can be of different kinds; they can be single words (*she, Martha, flatmates*); different sizes of noun phrases (*my [new] flatmates [from Italy]*). The subject of (9) is rather large and cumbersome, but we can formulate the question rule coherently only if we recognize that the subject of (9) is the whole sequence *my new flatmate who has won the Cordon Bleu cooking contest* and not some part of it. But complicated as this rule has become, it still needs some fine-tuning. Otherwise, how do we handle a sentence like (10), which does not contain an auxiliary verb? For some centuries English speakers have not formed questions in the manner of Othello ('Thinkst thou I'd make a life of jealousy . . .') by moving the lexical verb to the front of the sentence. In such cases as (10) we need to supply the appropriate form of *do*, as shown by (10a). But this also leads us to a yet more complex specification of our rule. Consider the ungrammatical sentence (13):

(13) *Do Martha cooks lasagne every Friday?

The verb *cook* in (10) is inflected with -*s* to mark present tense, and that present-tense marker must attach itself only to the auxiliary verb *do* in order to form the fully grammatical question (10a).

All the operations described above are required in order to construct a grammatical question. We here use the term 'grammatical' in a sense very different from that suggested by the prescriptive expression 'bad grammar'. A grammatical sentence in this more technical sense follows the rules of the language as it is used by its native speakers. These rules are followed unconsciously and, generally speaking, native speakers do not make mistakes of the kind illustrated by (11) and (13). However, young children take some time to acquire rules; one three-year-old asked, 'Did baby cried last night?' Second-language learners and speakers with strokes or head injuries can certainly experience problems with the grammar of questions. Although this rule is very much more complicated than the list of *dos* and *don'ts* which are the focus of prescriptive grammars because knowledge of it is unconscious, many speakers who are familiar with the rather different rules of prescriptive grammar simply do not know that it exists. This unconscious knowledge of a set of rules (we have looked at only one of these) which allows native speakers to produce grammatical sentences and to distinguish grammatical from ungrammatical sentences (we did this when we considered (11)) can be described as a *mental grammar*.

Prescriptive rules are never as complex as properly formulated descriptive rules, and are easily dealt with by descriptive grammars. For example, *different from/to* would simply be specified as options; the split infinitive would not be an issue since the infinitive form of the verb is *visit*, not *to visit*; 'Who am I speaking to?' would be viewed as a normal sentence following the rules of English.

Sentences like (14) and (15) are also subject to popular criticism:

(14) So I said to our Trish and our Sandra, 'Yous wash the dishes.'
(15) Was you watching the game when the rain started?

Unlike (1)–(6), which are regularly used by educated speakers and writers, both of these are characteristic of low-status speakers. They were recorded respectively in Belfast and London, although the grammatical patterns which they illustrate are found elsewhere. It is the low social status of these speakers, indexed by details of their language use, which seems in this case to form the basis of negative evaluation. In such a way is social class prejudice disguised as neutral intellectual commentary, and for this reason one linguist has described linguistic prescriptivism as the last open door to discrimination. But note that (14) makes a systematic distinction between 'you' (singular) and 'yous' (plural) similar to many languages of the world but lacking in Standard English. Thus, (14) cannot be argued to be in any sense linguistically impoverished (another common rationalization in defence of prescribed variants). Languages and dialects simply vary in the meaning distinctions they encode, regardless of their social status.

Note that (15) is a perfectly formulated question. Earlier in the history of English *was* and *were* in such sentences were acceptable alternatives (recall that the process of standardization has narrowed the range of socially and stylistically acceptable linguistic choices). But if we ask whether such sentences are 'slovenly' ('lacking in care and precision') we must surely concede that the care and precision needed to implement the question-formation rule is considerable, placing in perspective the triviality of requiring *were* with a plural subject.

Let us look finally at two sentences which seem to be subject to criticism for yet a different reason:

(16) Me and Andy went out to the park.
(17) it's very awkward/it's difficult mind you/with a class of thirty odd/occasionally with the second form/you'll get you know/ well we'll we'll have erm a debate/

Neither (16) nor (17) are clearly marked as belonging to a particular region, but between them they display a number of characteristics of informal spoken English. Uttered by an adolescent boy, (16) is criticized on the grounds that the wrong pronoun case (*me* instead of *I*) is used inside a conjoined phrase. Speakers are so conscious of this Latin-based prescription that even linguistically self-conscious and quite prescriptively minded individuals sometimes hypercorrect and use *I* where *me* is prescribed (a particularly large number of complaints about these patterns of pronoun use are received by the BBC). Thus Margaret Thatcher once announced, 'It is not for you and I to condemn the Malawi economy,' and Bill Clinton pleaded, 'Give Al Gore and I a chance.' But a systematic analysis of English grammar reveals underlying rules which permit variation between *me* and *I* only within conjoined phrases. Thus, adolescent boys do not habitually say 'Me went out to the park,' Clinton would not plead 'Give I a chance,' and not even Margaret Thatcher would have said 'It is not for I to condemn the Malawi economy.' With respect to *prescriptive* rules, there is often such a disparity between what speakers believe is correct and what they actually do; but *descriptive* rules are neither subject to violation nor are they part of our conscious knowledge of language.

Although conversation is often thought to be unstructured, ungrammatical and slovenly (presumably when judged against the norms of writing or formal speech), its complex organizational principles are quite different from those of planned spoken or written discourse; it is not simply spoken prose. Transcribed from a coffee-break conversation between two teachers, (17) is typical of informal conversation in its chunks (marked by slashes), which do not correspond to the sentences of written English. Also in evidence are fillers such as *erm*, hesitations (marked by full stops), repairs, repetitions, and discourse tokens such as *you know*, *mind you*. Most of these features are attributable to conversation's interactive, online mode of production, and the two discourse tokens function as 'participation markers', signalling to the interlocutor that interactional involvement or response is expected. Thus, it hardly seems appropriate to describe even the apparently unstructured utterance (17) as 'slovenly'.

So what are we to say in conclusion about our current myth? 'Bad grammar' is a cover term to describe a number of different kinds of English expressions. Some are widely used by educated speakers and writers but are outlawed by traditional prescriptions which are difficult to sustain; some appear to attract covert social prejudice by virtue of their association with low-status groups; and some follow the very characteristic but still rule-governed patterns of informal speech. All are perfectly grammatical, providing evidence of a complex body of rules which constitute mental grammars, the unconscious knowledge which speakers have of their own language. In comparison, the prescriptions which are recommended as 'good grammar' are revealed as at best marginal and frequently as unrealistic and trivial.

Sources and further reading

For details of the processes and consequences of prescriptivism, see Rosina Lippi-Green, *English with an Accent* (London: Routledge, 1997) and James Milroy and Lesley Milroy, *Authority in Language* (London: Routledge, 1985). For a humorous critique of some common prescriptions see Patricia O'Conner, *Woe is I: the grammarphobe's guide to better English in plain English* (New York: Grosset/Putnam, 1996). Mental grammars are discussed by Steven Pinker, *The Language Instinct* (London: Penguin, 1994) and for a standard descriptive grammar of English see Sidney Greenbaum, *The Oxford English Grammar* (Oxford: Oxford University Press, 1996).

MYTH 13

Black Children are Verbally Deprived

Walt Wolfram

Eloquent orators seem to abound in African-American culture. At religious meetings, political rallies and other social gatherings, speakers demonstrate dynamic, effectual discourse. From the powerful speeches of historic figures such as Frederick Douglass, through William Du Bois, Martin Luther King, Barbara Jordan and Jessie Jackson in the United States – and beyond North America to renowned African orators such as Kwame Nkrumah, Odumegwu Ojukwu and Desmond Tutu, this oratorical tradition is regularly practiced and highly valued. Even political and social opponents of these well-known black orators begrudgingly concede the power and utility of their speaking skills.

Quite clearly, verbal art is an integral, pervasive and highly valued component of black culture – on both a public and a personal level. Its influence on popular culture, through rappers, hip-hop culture and slang expressions is transparent, but it is more than that. Its roots are planted deep within the oral tradition of the African diaspora, and its branches extend to practically every sphere of communicative activity within black culture.

Given such an extensive and widely recognized oral tradition, it is indeed ironic to find young African-American children described in the educational literature as 'verbally deprived', 'language impoverished' or 'linguistically retarded'. Can these be children from the same culture we described above? If so, how can such contrasting pictures of language competence arise? And how do we reconcile the conflicting portraits of verbal richness and linguistic poverty? If nothing else, the lesson that emerges from the myth of African-American verbal deprivation shows how far from reality perceptions of language ability may wander. Or how much distortion can appear in a language portrait based on the angle of the observer.

As a backdrop for our discussion, we must admit that there are differences in varieties of English which may sometimes correlate with ethnicity. Some African-Americans simply do not sound the same as Anglo-Americans when they speak. When tape-recorded speech samples of working-class African-American and working-class Anglo-American are played, listeners identify with reasonable accuracy whether the speakers are black or white (about 80 per cent of the time in most listener tests based on relatively brief passages of natural speech).

The basis for these language differences is historically, socially and linguistically very natural and understandable. When people from different cultures come together, the languages reflecting these cultures mix and adapt. And when groups are segregated, isolated and excluded, they maintain and develop in different ways, thus enhancing language differences. So far so good – as over 6,000 world languages and multitudinous dialects of each of these distinct languages attest. But when different cultural groups are drastically unequal in their social and interactional relationships – and especially when one group has been dehumanized in comparison with the other – the environment for cultivating myths about these differences is fertile. The end result of these myths is to provide a justification for the differential power relations between the groups.

Myths about the language of African-Americans have, of course, changed as the perspective on the status of black Americans has shifted historically, but there is a common, unifying theme in the mythology, namely, *the linguistic inferiority principle*. According to this principle, the speech of a socially subordinate group will always be interpreted as inadequate by comparison with the socially dominant group. Explanations may vary, but the principle will be constant. Thus, when African-American speech is compared with the middle-class, Anglo-American norm, it will be considered linguistically deficient, although the explanations for the deficiency may vary.

In the days of slavery, when blacks were institutionally ascribed a status that was less than human, their speech was simply viewed as the communicative gibberish of a people inherently incapable of imitating the language of the ruling European-American classes. If a group of people is considered genetically deficient, what else is to be expected from their language? In various shapes and forms, the myth of genetic inferiority has persisted to some extent even in present-day society. Thus, there are still occasional references to the possible correlation of anatomical differences with racial differences, a throwback to the genetic basis for language differences among blacks and whites.

Myths correlating racial with linguistic differences are fairly easy to debunk logically and empirically. If race were truly a factor accounting for a dialect difference, then how would we explain the fact that African-Americans raised in an exclusively Anglo-American environment will sound indistinguishable from those of the surrounding speech community and vice versa? There is indisputable evidence from listener identification judgments that speakers will be identified with the language of their socialized community, not their racial classification.

Anatomically based explanations, for example, those based on lip size, are also easy to reject. For example, there is great diversity in lip size within both the white and black communities, yet no independent correlation with lip size and speech differences exists. White folks who have larger lips don't necessarily sound black, and blacks with smaller lips don't necessarily sound white. Besides, there is no indication from the world's races that lip size correlates in any way with the choice of particular sounds in a language.

But entrenched myths about language inadequacy are like a jack-in-the-box that keeps springing back up. So the exposure of one line of reasoning as objectively unjustified and illogical doesn't mean that linguistic equality will be attained. If the bottom-line belief is that one cultural group – and by extension, its language – is inferior to another, then another line of reasoning will simply replace the old one. Therefore, when nature is ruled out as a possible explanation for the distinctiveness of African-American speech, nurture may rise to the interpretive occasion. Genetically based myths have not died out completely in popular culture, but they have largely been supplanted by myths related to the social environment.

In some respects, the current set of myths tied to nurture is a more serious threat to the linguistic integrity of African-American speech than those based on nature, because they can be camouflaged in fashionable social and educational concern. In the process, the explanations for linguistic inferiority don't seem so blatantly racist as their precursors founded in genetic inferiority. But the semblance of respectability can actually present a more imposing obstacle to a valid understanding of black speech than conspicuously racist statements about anatomical differences accounting for linguistic differences.

In order for a myth to be nurtured in an increasingly educated society, it should be rooted in 'objective fact' and have a common-sense appeal. The verbal deprivation myth has done this by relying on the results of standardized tests and other formal assessment measures as 'the facts', then turning to conditions in the social environment to explain them. For example, the results of standardized language testing support the conclusion that 'disadvantaged children of almost every kind are typically one or two years retarded in language development' (Carl Bereiter, p. 196). The problem with the facts, however, is that they provide a distorted picture. The norms used as the basis for testing the speakers were derived from standard-English-speaking, middle-class Anglo children who speak a dialect different from their working-class cohorts. Therefore, the tests simply demonstrate a dialect difference between middle-class, standard dialects of English and other dialects.

No language expert would deny that African-American children who speak a variety of English different from the standard English norms used in the measuring instruments will score differently from – and lower than – those children who speak the language variety used as the basis for norming the test. A Canadian French child taking a test normed on Parisian French or a Spanish-speaking South-American child taking a Spanish test normed on Castilian Spanish spoken in Spain would suffer a similar fate in their 'objective' test scores. If standard dialect speakers were given a test using normative, uniquely African-American language structures, they would suffer a comparable fate. Of course, when one group is economically and socially dominant over another, differences will always be interpreted in a way that supports the asymmetrical socio-economic, socio-political and socio-educational status quo. In such a comparative scenario, it is easy to see how cultural and language differences will be interpreted as deficits. So it is just a matter of explaining why these deficits exist. The seeds of language deprivation are firmly planted through 'facts'; now all that is needed is an explanation that will allow the principle of linguistic inferiority to be nurtured properly.

Interpretative explanations that sustain the myth of the linguistically deprived black child appeal to the process of language learning, the nature of language patterning and the situations used to demonstrate language capability. With respect to language learning, models of parenting in general and verbal interaction between caretakers and children in particular are cited as support for the alleged verbal deprivation of African-American children. Some middle-class parents take a fairly proactive, although highly selective role in teaching young children new words and directly modeling speech. By the same token, some working-class parents may not be as proactive in directly modeling language in this way. Looking at this situation, educational psychologists have maintained that working-class black children do not get adequate verbal stimulation from their caretakers by comparison with their middle-class cohorts and, therefore, they end up language-handicapped.

At first glance, this line of reasoning seems sensible – if one assumes that parents and caretakers must play a proactive role for language acquisition to take place. But as it turns out, this is a totally erroneous assumption. There is absolutely no basis for maintaining that language acquisition comes through direct parental initiative; in fact, there is a lot of evidence against it. The capacity for language is a unique attribute of the human mind, and there is overwhelming evidence that all that is needed for normal language development to take place is exposure to a social environment where people use language to interact meaningfully. Anyone who has ever been in a working-class black home knows that verbal interaction is profuse and productive. Children interact with each other and adults interact with each other and with the children. Certainly, there is extensive verbal interaction to provide models for language acquisition, and any claim to the contrary would be totally absurd.

There are a number of different models for interaction in the acquisition of normal language. Surveys of language socialization across the world's cultures indicate that parent–child, adult care-taker–child, and older sibling– and peer–child interactions all work effectively in modeling the language necessary for acquisition. Regardless of the model, all children acquiring language have a basic language system by the age of five or six, with minor refinements taking place for another five or six years. In fact, surveys of language socialization models in languages around the world indicate that the parent–child interaction model is a minority one. But that's not the essential point; the important fact is that there are different social interactional models for providing the necessary input for the stimulation of normal language learning. A parent's proactive role in teaching language may make the parent feel involved and responsible, but it has little to do with the ultimate acquisition of normal language. This is fortunate; if it were not so, the vast majority of the world's languages would never be acquired adequately.

The myth of language deprivation is also supported by a mistaken understanding about language patterning. There is a popular perception that standard dialects have regular patterns – the 'rules' of language – and that structures that differ from these rules violate the basic patterns of language. From this perspective, non-standard varieties involve violations of the standard dialect but no rules of their own. This is the *grammaticality myth*, which holds that any structure not in conformity with standard English norms is designated 'ungrammatical'. This myth lumps together cases of true ungrammaticality, where the basic patterns for forming sentences in a language are indeed violated, and social judgments about differently patterned language forms.

For example, an English speaker uttering a sentence such as *dog the barks* would violate a basic sequencing rule of English grammar in which articles regularly come before nouns rather than after them – a case of true ungrammaticality for English. However, the grammaticality myth holds that sentences such as *They be talking all the time,* *They didn't do nothing to nobody about nothing,* and *She nice* would be considered as cases of ungrammatical language as well. While these sentences may certainly be socially disfavored, they are rigorously patterned. For example, the use of *be* in sentences such as *They be talking all the time* or *Sometimes my ears be itching* uniquely marks a 'habitual activity' as opposed to a single-point activity in African-American Vernacular English. It is rigorously constrained in its patterning – different from standard English but every bit as patterned as any comparable structure in the standard variety. Observations of speakers' use and tests of preferences for sentences with *be* indicate that speakers of African-American Vernacular English will systematically select *be* for habitual contexts such as *Sometimes they be doing it* but not for single-time contexts such as *They be doing it right now.* Unfortunately, following the grammaticality myth, this regular patterning is not even considered to be a possibility. Instead, social acceptability has become equated with linguistic patterning; thus, a social judgment is translated into a misguided notion of language organization. No one is saying that this structure should be considered standard English – just that its linguistic integrity stands apart from its social assessment.

Some language differences may even be interpreted in terms of logic. Thus, the use of multiple negatives such as *They didn't do nothing,* which is used in African-American Vernacular English as in many other vernacular varieties of English, may be interpreted as an indication of a flawed logic system – the *logicality myth.* In a fanciful appeal to formal logical operations in which negatives can cancel each other under certain conditions, it is sometimes maintained that speakers who use multiple negatives lapse into illogical language use. But formal, syllogistic reasoning is quite different from the grammatical manifestations of basic language propositions, including negation, where there are varied linguistic manifestations of basic propositions. In fact, many languages regularly and exclusively use multiple negation in certain types of constructions. Compare, for example, the French sentence *Je ne sais rien* 'I don't know nothing,' the Spanish sentence *No hace nada* 'S/he isn't doing nothing,' or even older English constructions such as *There was **no** man **nowhere** so virtuous*, where multiple negatives were the standard norm. Unless one is prepared to say that French, Spanish, the English of respected authors like Chaucer and many other languages of the world are innately illogical in their organization, we must concede that appealing to logic in support of the deficiency of African-American Vernacular English is, somewhat ironically, a quite illogical line of reasoning itself.

Similarly, it has been argued that verbless sentences such as *She nice* or *The dog brown* may be indicative of a cognitive breakdown in denoting relationships of identity. But as it turns out, the juxtaposition of items in these constructions is a simple variant for linking predicate constructions, including predicate adjectives such as *She nice* or location constructions such as *She in the house*. Languages like Russian, Thai and many others use such constructions, since the verb in these kinds of construction turns out to be redundant. Appeals to logic may have a very strong common-sense appeal, but the logic of these appeals for language organization is fatally flawed.

Finally, we should say something about the perceptions of the 'nonverbal' African-American child. This classification has been made by some educators who observed that some African-American children may say little or nothing when spoken to by adults under certain kinds of conditions. The typical situation on which these conclusions are based involves an adult attempting to elicit conversation in what seems – at least for the adult – to be a relatively innocuous and non-threatening situation. But consider the typical scenario in which a friendly adult sits across from a child in an institutional setting and asks the child simply to 'tell me everything you can about the fire engine on the table.' The situation is laden with values about language use, including the value of verbosity (the more you speak the better), obvious information (there is value in describing objects that the questioner already knows about) and consequences for providing information (what a child tells will not be held against the child), to say nothing of the asymmetrical power relations between the adult stranger and child in a relatively alien, institutional setting. The same child who says virtually nothing about the fire engine in this social situation may, in fact, be highly animated and verbal when playing with the fire engine in her home on the floor with her playmates. The appearance of nonverbalness is just that – an appearance created by the artificial testing conditions under which language is sometimes collected for the purposes of assessment. Given the actual value of verbal presentation and repartee as discussed earlier, the myth of the nonverbal black child is perhaps the most ironic twist of all in the assessment of African-Americans' language ability.

In challenging the myth of black language deprivation, I am not trying to say that the language of the home and community is appropriate for the particularized and socialized uses of language in education and other kinds of public institutions. There is an academic register necessary for carrying out certain kinds of educational routines, just as there is a language register for carrying out certain kinds of legal routines. In fact, there are lots of different situations and domains for language that call for specialized language uses, and our participation in particular institutions in society necessitates that we be familiar with the registers associated with them. But these specialized uses of language have nothing to do with basic language capability.

In some respects, no myth about African-Americans seems more absurd than the myth of verbal deprivation. All the evidence indicates that black culture is a highly verbal culture which values the development of verbal skills. Unfortunately, relationships of social and political inequality can lead to the dismissal of even the most obvious reality in order to mold language perceptions in conformity with the inferiority principle. Rather than being labeled as verbally deprived, African-Americans ought to be thanked for contributing to daily conversation with words, phrases and other manners of speaking that enrich our language and our lives.

Sources and further reading

The quote on language disadvantage is taken from Carl Bereiter, 'Academic instruction and preschool children', in Richard Corbin and Muriel Crosby, *Language Programs for the Disadvantaged* (Champaign, IL: National Council of Teachers of English, 1965). Some of the contributions of African-Americans to American speech through various phrases are cited in Geneva Smitherman, *Black Talk: Words and Phrases from the Hood to the Amen Corner* (Middleborough, MA: The Country Press, 1995). William Labov's 'The logic of non-standard English', in *Language in the Inner City: Studies in the Black English Vernacular* (Philadelphia, PA: The University of Pennsylvania Press, 1972) remains a classic article attacking the language deprivation myth.

MYTH 14

Double Negatives are Illogical

Jenny Cheshire

> *Nothing shows why*
> *At this unique distance from isolation,*
> *It becomes still more difficult to find*
> *Words at once true and kind,*
> *Or not untrue and not unkind.*
> *–Philip Larkin, 'Talking in Bed'*

An' when they be saying if you good, you goin' t'heaven, tha's bullshit,
'cause you ain't goin' to no heaven, 'cause there ain't no heaven for you
to go to. –fifteen-year-old black youth from Harlem

You won't get nothing for dinner if you don't come in and clear up your
mess. –adult woman from Hackney, East London

It never occurred to me to doubt that your work would not advance our
common object in the highest degree. –Charles Darwin

There are three types of double negative here, each of which is from
time to time condemned as illogical. Fowler's *Guide to Good Usage*
claims that the type illustrated by Darwin's sentence is a 'fuzzy error'
that occurs when people don't know exactly how to handle negatives.
George Orwell said that the first kind (*not* plus a negative adjective)
should be 'laughed out of existence'. But it is the second kind, where
there is a negative verb (*ain't* and *won't* in the examples here) and a
negative word such as *no*, *nothing* or *no one*, that arouses the strongest
feelings. It was one of the top ten complaints sent in 1986 to the BBC
Radio 4 series *English Now* after listeners had been invited to nominate

the three points of grammatical usage they most disliked. Those who wrote in did more than simply dislike their chosen items: they said that they 'made their blood boil', 'gave a pain to their ear', 'made them shudder' and 'appalled' them. Double negatives, it seems, cause a great deal of suffering, so it is worth investigating the nature of the problem.

If you ask people *why* they object to double negatives, they usually point to logic, where there is a long tradition of assuming that two people refer to mathematics, where 'minus two minus minus two equals zero,' with the two minuses effectively turning the first part of the equation into 'minus two plus two.' From these analogies, some people argue, it follows that two negatives in the same sentence must also cancel each other out, turning *there ain't no heaven for you to go to* into *there IS a heaven for you to go*. In the same way, they say, the two negatives in *not untrue* should, according to the rules of logic, mean simply 'true'.

It is very simple to show, however, that this is not a sensible way to argue. If we really want to apply the principles of mathematics to language we must also consider utterances where there are not two but three negatives, like *I didn't give nothing to no one*. If two negatives cancel each other out, sentences such as this one are clearly negative, for there will still be one negative left after two of them have been cancelled out. But which one is left? *Didn't, nothing* or *no one*? Unlike the figures of mathematics, words in language have meaning, so if we cancel some of the negatives we change the meaning of the sentence. If we apply the rules of logic to *I didn't give nothing to no one*, then, should we decide that the utterance means 'I gave something to no one', or 'I gave nothing to someone'? Things get more complicated still if we consider what the affirmative version would be: *I gave something to everyone*? *I gave everything to someone*? Or *I gave something to someone*? The problem is that if we want seriously to apply the rules of logic to language, we cannot think only in terms of negation. We have to take account of other distinctions that are important in logic. Words like *nothing, no* or *no one* are the negative equivalents of what logicians term 'universal quantifiers', like *everything* and *everyone*; but they are also the negative equivalents of 'existential quantifiers' like *something* and *someone*. Issues concerning the logical interaction between negation and quantification have kept philosophers busy since the time of Aristotle and before. When we have two negatives to deal with, then, the question is not just whether or not they are illogical, but precisely which logical issues are involved and how they interrelate with each other and with the rest of the utterance.

In view of all these complexities, it is fortunate that it is very rarely appropriate to think in terms of logic when looking at language use. We do not utter phrases like *you ain't going to no heaven* in isolation, nor do we ponder over the meaning of what our interlocutor has said in the way that philosophers do, to decide whether or not the negative sentence conforms to the rules of logic. If we say something that is negative it is because we want to deny something that someone has said or implied to us: for example, the young man in the example from Harlem was denying what people had told him about going to heaven if you're good, as his previous remarks make clear. As for potential problems of ambiguity, these are very rare in speech because the person we are communicating with is right there with us. If there do happen to be any ambiguities about whether we mean *something* or *nothing*, or whether we really mean to be negative or not, we can sort out the problem straight away. Ambiguity may be more of a problem in writing, but a large body of research has shown that in any case negatives occur far more often in spoken language than written language.

Quite apart from the fact that the context will almost always clarify any possible ambiguity, as soon as you look at the way we use negatives in conversation it becomes obvious that we rarely, in fact, work with a simple two-way distinction between 'negative' and 'not negative'. It *is* necessary to think this way when programming a computer: computers need to react to simple two-way distinctions like 'negative' or 'not negative' because they can't – yet – handle anything more complex. Human beings, however, are not computers. In order to gather some examples of negative utterances I went out this morning, on a typically grey London day, and said to the first ten people I chatted to 'I think it looks like rain today.' Some agreed that it did.

The six who didn't think it would rain replied in the ways shown below.

> **Do you think it looks like rain?**
> oh no I don't think so
> definitely not, it was like this yesterday and it didn't rain
> no no, it's going to be fine later
> not to me it doesn't
> well they didn't forecast rain on the radio this morning
> no but I wish it would, then I could go to work by car
>   without feeling guilty
> maybe, maybe not

These responses are typical of the way we use language. If we want to negate something that someone has said to us, it is perfectly possible to use a bare negative, saying simply *no*. More often than not, though, we will do more than this. We may hedge our negative so that it is not too definite (*no I don't think so*) or we may make the negative very emphatic (*definitely not*), perhaps with two negatives (*no no*, or *not to me it doesn't*) – which do not, by the way, cancel each other out. We may say whether our denial is based on our own opinion (*not to me it doesn't*), or on some more justifiable authority, such as the radio weather forecast, or we may reveal how we feel about the possibility of rain (*I wish it would*). The possibilities are endless. Replies can even be both negative and non-negative at the same time (*maybe, maybe not*). Unlike computers, when we communicate with each other we do not deal only in simple two-way distinctions: there are many other important aspects of meaning that we convey at the same time as the factual information.

Phrases such as *not untrue* and *not unkind* also reflect our needs, as human beings, to go beyond simple two-way distinctions. If you stop and think about it, you will probably agree that there are very few distinctions in the real world that are clearly either one thing or the other. Most of the time we are dealing with something in between. A new neighbour, for example, can be friendly or unfriendly, but there is also a neutral possibility and an infinite number of graduations between the two extremes. We can extend the extremes, with a 'very friendly' neighbour or neighbour who is 'not friendly at all'. 'Opposite' meanings are best seen as forming a continuum rather than as being mutually exclusive alternatives; and using two negatives (like *not unfriendly*) allows us to situate ourselves somewhere within the middle ground but without necessarily saying exactly where. Many of our conventional expressions show that people like to contrive subtle distinctions even between pairs of words that should, strictly speaking, be mutually exclusive. Take the words *alive* and *dead*: if we are dead, then we cannot, in principle, also be alive, and there can be no half-way stage. Yet there are well-used phrases such as *more dead than alive* or *only half-alive*. Not surprisingly, the only words that we don't treat in this apparently illogical way are words that refer to mathematical principles; a number like 3 is 'odd' and 4 is 'even', and no one tries to draw any fine distinctions between odd numbers and even numbers. This is because here we really are dealing with the rules of mathematics. In real life we are not.

It is interesting that people react in contradictory ways to the *not untrue* type of double negative. George Orwell objected that it gives 'bland statements an appearance of profundity', allowing people to sit on the fence, in the middle ground between one extreme and the other – which is probably why it is used so frequently by British politicians. The satirical magazine *Private Eye* has a mock diary entry for the British Prime Minister which is peppered with double negatives of this kind. Orwell's suggested cure for people who like to use these double negatives was that they should memorize the ludicrous sentence *A not unblack dog was chasing a not unsmall rabbit across a not ungreen field.*

Others, however, neither object nor laugh but see double negatives as elegant. It is considered good style to write *neither . . . nor*, as I just did. Erasmus thought that double negatives were 'graceful' and 'elegant', recommending the use of *not ungrateful* for 'very grateful' and *not vulgarly* for 'singularly'. In the eighteenth century some grammarians warned against using double negatives on the grounds that they were illogical or in bad taste, but others were in favour of them. One American grammarian, Lindley Murray, censored them

The Secret DIARY OF JOHN MAJOR aged 47¾

Monday

I was not inconsiderably sorry to see all the news placards this morning. They all had in very big letters "NEW TORY SEX SCANDAL".

–*Private Eye*, no. 866, 24.2.95, p. 21

Wednesday

I do not know whether to be very not inconsiderably annoyed or quite not inconsiderably pleased. This morning I saw on the hotel's CNN News that no sooner have I turned my back than the great economic recovery has come to an end. This only goes to show how wrong I was to leave Mr Heseltine in charge.

–*Private Eye*, no. 879, 25.8.95, p. 19

as illogical but then went on to claim that they formed 'a pleasing and delicate variety of expression'. If there is anything illogical about double negatives, then, it is people's reactions to them: some hate them, some love them; some, like Murray, both hate and love them; some people laugh at them whilst others, like the BBC correspondents, are appalled.

Most people, however, happily utter double negatives without, we must assume, realizing the emotional havoc they could be causing and without worrying about being illogical. They are right not to worry, for two reasons. First, the tests that linguists use to determine whether or not a sentence is negative would identify all the examples at the beginning of this chapter as unambiguously negative, despite the double negatives. Linguists identify the principles underlying language structure by analysing languages in terms of their own rules and regularities, recognizing that linguistic structure does not necessarily follow the rules of logic. One such linguistic test for negation is to try adding a 'not even' phrase to a sentence. For example, we can say *you ain't going to no heaven, not even if you repent of all your sins* – or, if you prefer, *you aren't going to no heaven, not even if you repent of all your sins* – but it makes no sense to say *you are going to heaven, not even if you repent of all your sins*. The latter sentence, then, is not negative, but the first two are, despite their double negatives. There are no linguistic grounds, then, for deciding that the two negatives have cancelled each other out. Secondly, the system of negation in English has never, in any case, been one in which two negatives cancel each other to make an affirmative. On the contrary, in Old English negatives tended to accumulate in a sentence, reinforcing each other. Multiple negatives are also frequent in Chaucer and Shakespeare's work, and in later writers too.

He forbad aet mon nane faeste boc ne leorde. (from *Orosius*)
He forbade anyone (not) to read (not) any book.

But nevere gronte he at no strook but oon. (Chaucer, *Canterbury Tales*)
But he never groaned at any of the blows except one.

I have one heart, one bosom, and one truth
And that no woman has; nor never none
Shall mistress be of it, save I alone. (*Twelfth Night* III.i.172–4)

One negative encouraged another, it seems, and most scholars agree that the more negatives there were in a sentence, the more emphatic the denial or rejection. Double negation is found in the majority of the world's languages: in French, for example, *I don't want anything* is translated by *je ne veux rien*, with two negatives, *ne* and *rien*. Spanish, Russian, Hungarian, Arabic and most other languages of the world follow the same pattern, which looks very much, therefore, like a natural pattern for language. For English, double negatives are attested in all the dialects, whether rural or urban, southern hemisphere or northern hemisphere; they occur in African-American English and in all the English creoles. It is only in the standard variety of English that double negatives have fallen out of favour. As far as it is possible to tell, their decline seems to have taken place during the eighteenth century. This was the period when grammarians attempted to establish a set of norms for good usage: in the case of double negatives they tended to share the views of the BBC listeners, as we have seen. The development of a specific style for formal written prose at that time may also have encouraged the decline of double negatives, for in writing the risk of ambiguity does exist, since our interlocutor is not present and it is impossible to use intonation or stress to make our meaning crystal clear. The eighteenth century was also a time when 'polite' society, in Britain at least, was striving to develop a 'cultivated' style of speech. It became conventional in polite circles to use a detached impersonal style, so it would not have been surprising if their members had stripped their speech of the emphasis conveyed by multiple negatives. In the same way, today, many 'cultivated' speakers favour understatement by saying 'rather good' instead of 'very good', and express detachment by using the pronoun 'one' where others might prefer to say 'I' or 'you'.

The outcome is that the different types of double negatives have come to be used by varying groups of people. Those of us who like to reflect on usage tend to notice double negatives when they occur and to pass judgement on them, but – perhaps unconsciously – our judgements often reflect the social associations that the double negatives have for us. The *not unimportant* kind has become typical of careful, formal speech: this is the type that is played on by poets and parodied by satirists. It gives rise to mixed reactions, as we've seen. The type illustrated in the Charles Darwin extract occurs more often in writing than in speech and does, it is true, require concentration to sort out the intended meaning; this is the type of double negation that Fowler claimed to be a fuzzy error. The main objections, however, are reserved for double negatives of the *I don't want nothing* type, which nowadays are used not by politicians, potential poet laureates or scientists, but by Harlem youths, London East Enders and other groups in the community whose ancestors escaped the demands of polite society and the prescriptions of grammarians. These double negatives represent the survival of a long-established pattern of negation in English and a natural pattern of negation in language generally. They might be recognized in this way if our greatest playwrights still used them. But as it is, they are stigmatized.

I conclude, then, with a phrase which some readers will find ridiculous but which others will see as graceful and elegant: double negatives are, very definitely, not illogical.

Sources and further reading

The example from Philip Larkin is taken from Laurence R. Horn, *A Natural History of Negation* (London and Chicago: University of Chicago Press, 1989, p. 296). There is a section in this book devoted to double negation (section 5.1.3, pp. 296–308). The example from Harlem comes from William Labov's chapter 'The logic of nonstandard English' (p. 215), from his book *Language in the Inner City* (Philadelphia: University of Pennsylvania Press, 1972, pp. 130–96). The chapter 'Negative attraction and negative concord', in the same book (pp. 201–40) gives a detailed linguistic analysis of double negation and other types of negation in English, including discussion of the interrelations between negation and quantification. The example from

Charles Darwin is quoted by Otto Jespersen in his classic work *Negation in English and Other Languages* (Copenhagen: Andr. Fred Høst and Son, 1917). Linguistic tests for negation are discussed by Edward S. Klima, 'Negation in English', in *The Structure of Language: Readings in the philosophy of language*, Jerry A. Fodor and Jerrold J. Katz (eds.) (Englewood Cliffs, NJ: Prentice-Hall Inc., 1964, pp. 246–323). Further discussion of negation in language and logic can be found in Östen Dahl's contribution, 'Negation', to *Syntax: An international handbook of contemporary research* (Berlin: Walter de Gruyter, pp. 914–23). Gunnel Tottie's *Negation in English Speech and Writing: A variationist study* (London: Academic Press, 1991) gives a detailed analysis of the quantity and the types of negation that have been attested in educated spoken and written modern English. For the history of double negatives in English, see Daniel W. Noland, 'A diachronic survey of English negative concord' (*American Speech* 66 (1991), pp. 171–80); and for a brief history of negation in English generally, see Jenny Cheshire's 'English negation from an interactional perspective', in *The Sociolinguistics Reader*, Volume 1, edited by Peter Trudgill and Jenny Cheshire (London: Arnold, 1998). The role of politeness and delicacy in determining the form of standard English grammar is discussed in Laurence Klein's chapter ' "Politeness" as linguistic ideology in late-seventeenth- and early-eighteenth-century England', in *Towards a Standard English 1600–1800*, Dieter Stein and Ingrid Tieken-Boon van Ostade (eds.) (Berlin and New York: Mouton de Gruyter, 1993, pp. 31–50).

MYTH 15

TV Makes People Sound the Same

J. K. Chambers

We sociolinguists often find ourselves discussing changes that are taking place in the speech communities around us. The changes themselves are usually crystal clear – for example, *dived* is being replaced as the past-tense form by *dove*, as in the case study I discuss below. And the way those changes are being realized – *actualized*, we usually say – in the speech of the community is also quite clear in most cases. Using methods that are by now well tested, we can discover the frequency of innovative forms like *dove* in the speech of twenty-year-olds and contrast that with its frequency in the speech of fifty-year-olds or eighty-year-olds, as I also do in the case study below. We can compare women with men, or people from different neighborhoods, or people of different social and occupational status, sifting through the evidence until we are confident we know who is leading the change and where it is heading.

But it is often much more difficult for us to pinpoint the reasons for the change – its *motivation*. The reasons behind linguistic changes are almost always very subtle. The number of possibilities is enormous, taking in such factors as motor economy in the physiology of pronunciation, adolescent rebellion from childhood norms, grammatical fine-tuning by young adults making their way in the marketplace, fads, fancies and fashions, and much more. All these things operate beneath consciousness, of course, making their detection even harder. You can't see them or measure them; you can only infer them.

Besides that, linguistic change is mysterious at its core. Why should languages change at all? From the beginning of recorded history (and presumably before that), people have been replacing perfectly serviceable norms in their speech with new ones. Why not keep the old, familiar norms? No one knows. All we know for certain is that language change is as inevitable as the tides.

So, very often we are forced to admit that the motivation for a change is unclear, or uncertain, or undetectable. We can often point to trends – sometimes even to age-old tendencies (again, as in the change of *dived* to *dove* below) that suddenly accelerated and became the new norm. But exactly why that tendency toward change arose and, more baffling, exactly why it accelerated at that time and in that place is a very difficult question, one of the most resistant mysteries of linguistics.

Knowing all this, we are perpetually surprised to find that very often the people we are discussing these linguistic changes with – our students, colleagues in other departments, audiences at lectures, newspaper reporters, dinner-party guests – know exactly why the changes are taking place. It's because of television, they say. It's the mass media – the movies and the radio, but especially the television. Television is the primary hypothesis for the motivation of any sound change for everyone, it seems, except the sociolinguists studying it. The sociolinguists see some evidence for the mass media playing a role in the spread of vocabulary items. But at the deeper reaches of language change – sound changes and grammatical changes – the media have no significant effect at all.

The sociolinguistic evidence runs contrary to the deep-seated popular conviction that the mass media influence language profoundly. The idea that people in isolated places learn to speak standard English from hearing it in the media turns up, for instance, as a presupposition in this passage from a 1966 novel by Harold Horwood set in a Newfoundland fishing outport:

The people of Caplin Bight, when addressing a stranger from the mainland, could use almost accentless English, learned from listening to the radio, but in conversation among themselves there lingered the broad twang of ancient British dialects that the fishermen of Devon and Cornwall and the Isle of Guernsey had brought to the coast three or four centuries before.

The novelist's claim that the villagers could speak urban, inland middle-class English – presumably that is what he means by 'almost accentless English' – from hearing it on the radio is pure fantasy. It is linguistic science-fiction.

A more subtle fictional example, this one set in the apple-growing Annapolis Valley in Nova Scotia, will prove more instructive for us in trying to get to the roots of the myth. In a 1952 novel by Ernest Buckler, *The Mountain and the Valley*, the young narrator observes certain changes in his rural neighbors. His description of those changes is characteristically grandiloquent:

And the people lost their wholeness, the valid stamp of their indigenousness . . . In their speech (freckled with current phrases of jocularity copied from the radio), and finally in themselves, they became dilute.

Here, the author does not claim that the mass media are directly responsible for the dilution of regional speech. He does, however, conjoin the two notions. The dialect is losing its local 'stamp', he says, and incidentally it is 'freckled' with catch-phrases from the network sitcoms.

Beyond a doubt, mass communication diffuses catch-phrases. At the furthest reaches of the broadcast beam one hears echoes of Sylvester the Cat's 'Sufferin' succotash', or Monty Python's 'upper-class twit', or Fred Flintstone's 'Ya-ba da-ba doo'. When an adolescent says something that his friends consider unusually intelligent, the friends might look at one another and say, 'Check out the brains on Brett' – although the speaker is not named Brett. That line is a verbatim quotation from the 1994 film *Pulp Fiction*. Or they might compliment someone and then take it back emphatically: 'Those are nice mauve socks you're wearing – NOT!' That phrase originated on an American television program, *Saturday Night Live*, in 1978, but it went almost unnoticed until it came into frequent use in one recurring segment of the same show twelve years later. From there, it disseminated far and wide in a juvenile movie spin off called *Wayne's World* in 1992. Once it gained world-wide currency, other media picked it up, charting its source and tracking its course and spreading it even further. But its very trendiness doomed it. It was over-used, and a couple of years later it was a fading relic.

Such catch-phrases are more ephemeral than slang, and more self-conscious than etiquette. They belong for the moment of their currency to the most superficial linguistic level.

Unlike sound changes and grammatical changes, these lexical changes based on the media are akin to affectations. People notice them when others use them, and they know their source. And they apparently take them as prototypes for other changes in language. If the mass media can popularize words and expressions, the reasoning goes, then presumably they can also spread other kinds of linguistic changes.

It comes as a great surprise, then, to discover that there is no evidence for television or the other popular media disseminating or influencing sound changes or grammatical innovations. The evidence against it, to be sure, is indirect. Mostly it consists of a lack of evidence where we would expect to find strong positive effects.

For one thing, we know that regional dialects continue to diverge from standard dialects despite the exposure of speakers of those dialects to television, radio, movies and other media. The best-studied dialect divergence is occurring in American inner cities, where the dialects of the most segregated African-Americans sound less like their white counterparts with respect to certain features now than they did two or three generations ago. Yet these groups are avid consumers of mass media. William Labov observes that in inner-city Philadelphia the 'dialect is drifting further away' from other dialects despite 4–8 hours daily exposure to standard English on television and in schools.

For another thing, we have abundant evidence that mass media cannot provide the stimulus for language acquisition. Hearing children of deaf parents cannot acquire language from exposure to radio or television. Case studies now go back more than twenty-five years, when the psycholinguist Ervin-Tripp studied children who failed to begin speaking until they were spoken to in common, mundane situations by other human beings. More recently, Todd and Aitchison charted the progress of a boy named Vincent, born of deaf parents who communicated with him by signing, at which he was fully competent from infancy. His parents also encouraged him to watch television regularly, expecting it to provide a model for the speech skills they did not have. But Vincent remained speechless. By the time he was exposed to normal spoken intercourse at age three, his speaking ability was undeveloped and his capacity for acquiring speech was seriously impaired. He had not even gained passive skills from all the televised talk he had heard.

Finally, the third kind of evidence against media influence on language change comes from instances of global language changes. One of the best-studied global changes is the intonation pattern called uptalk or high rising terminals, in which declarative statements occur with yes/no question intonation. This feature occurs mainly (but not exclusively) in the speech of people under forty; it is clearly an innovation of the present generation. Astoundingly, in the few decades of its existence it has spread to virtually all English-speaking communities in the world; it has been studied in Australia, Canada, England, New Zealand and the United States. Its pragmatics are clear: it is used when the speaker is establishing common ground with the listener as the basis for the conversation (*Hello. I'm a student in your phonetics tutorial?*), and when the speaker is seeking silent affirmation of some factor that would otherwise require explanation before the conversation could continue (*Our high-school class is doing an experiment on photosynthesis?*). Its uses have generalized to take in situations where the pragmatics are not quite so clear (as in *Hello. My name is Robin?*).

So we know how it is used, but we do not know why it came into being or how it spread so far. Many people automatically assume that a change like this could never be so far-reaching unless it were abetted by the equally far-reaching media. But nothing could be further from the truth. In fact, the one social context where uptalk is almost never heard is in broadcast language. To date, uptalk is not a feature of any newsreader or weather analyst's speech on any national network anywhere in the world. More important, it is also not a regular, natural (unselfconscious) feature of any character's speech in sitcoms, soap operas, serials or interview shows anywhere in the world. Undoubtedly it soon will be, but that will only happen when television catches up with language change. Not vice versa.

Another telling instance comes from southern Ontario, the most populous part of Canada, where numerous changes are taking place in standard Canadian English and many of them are in the direction of north-eastern American English as spoken just across the Niagara gorge. The assumption of media influence is perhaps to be expected because of the proximity of the border on three sides and also because American television has blanketed Ontario since 1950. But closer inspection shows the assumption is wrong.

One example of the changes is *dove*, as in *The loon dove to the floor of the lake*. The standard past tense was *dived*, the weak (or regular) form. Indeed, *dived* was the traditional form, used for centuries. But in Canada (and elsewhere, as we shall see) *dove* competed with it in general use in the first half of this century, and now has all but replaced it completely.

The progress of this grammatical change is graphically evident in Figure 1, which shows the usage of people over seventy at the left-hand end and compares it with younger people decade by decade all the way down to teenagers (14–19) at the right-hand end. These results come from a survey of almost a thousand Canadians in 1992. People born in the 1920s and 1930s – the sixty- and seventy-year-olds in the figure – usually said *dived*, but people born in succeeding decades increasingly said *dove*. Since the 1960s, when the thirty-year-olds were born, about 90 per cent say *dove*, to the point where some teenagers today have never heard *dived* and consider it 'baby talk' when it is drawn to their attention.

The newer form, *dove*, is unmistakably American. More than 95 per cent of the Americans surveyed at the Niagara border say *dove*. In fact, *dove* has long been recognized by dialectologists as a character-istically Northern US form. In Canada, it had been a minority form since at least 1857, when a Methodist minister published a complaint about its use in what he called 'vulgar' speech.

Is the Canadian change a result of television saturation from America? Hardly. The past tense of the verb *dive* is not a frequently used word, and so the possibility of Canadians hearing it once in

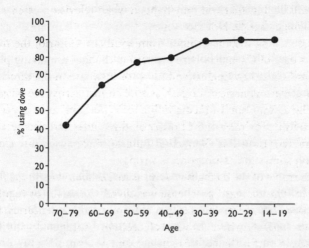

Figure 1: Percentage of Canadians who use dove *rather than* dived

American broadcasts is very slim, let alone hearing it so frequently as to become habituated to it. More important, there is evidence that *dove* is replacing *dived* in many other places besides Canada. For example, students in Texas now use *dove* almost exclusively, whereas few of their parents and none of their grandparents used this (formerly) Northern form.

The fact that these language changes are spreading at the same historical moment as the globalization of mass media should not be construed as cause and effect. It may be that the media diffuse tolerance toward other accents and dialects. The fact that standard speech reaches dialect enclaves from the mouths of anchorpersons, sitcom protagonists, color commentators and other admired people presumably adds a patina of respectability to any regional changes that are standardizing. But the changes themselves must be conveyed in face-to-face interactions among peers.

One of the modern changes of even greater social significance than the media explosion is high mobility. Nowadays, more people meet face to face across greater distances than ever before. The talking heads on our mass media sometimes catch our attention but they never engage us in dialogue. Travelers, salesmen, neighbors and work-mates from distant places speak to us and we hear not only what they say but how they say it. We may unconsciously borrow some features of their speech and they may borrow some of ours. That is quite normal. But it takes real people to make an impression. For us no less than for Vincent.

Sources and further reading

I previously discussed the influence of mass media and other post-modern factors on language change in 'Sociolinguistic dialectology' (in *American Dialect Research*, Dennis Preston (ed.), Amsterdam: John Benjamins, 1993, especially pp. 137–42). Detailed explanations of the social motivations for linguistic change may be found in my book *Sociolinguistic Theory: Linguistic variation and its social significance* (Oxford: Blackwell, 1995, especially Chs. 2 and 4).

The two novels cited are *Tomorrow will be Sunday*, Harold Horwood (Toronto: Paperjacks, 1966) and *The Mountain and the Valley*, Ernest Buckler (Toronto: McClelland and Stewart, 1961).

William Labov's observation of dialect divergence despite intensive media exposure comes from his presentation on 'The transmission of linguistic traits across and within communities', at the 1984 Symposium on Language Transmission and Change, Center for Advanced Study in the Behavioral Sciences.

Case studies of the hearing children of deaf parents may be found in Susan Ervin-Tripp, 'Some strategies for the first two years' (in *Cognition and the Acquisition of Language*, New York: Academic Press, 1973, pp. 261–86) and 'Learning language the hard way', by P. Todd and J. Aitchison in the journal *First Language* 1 (1980), pp. 122–40. The case of Vincent is also summarized in Aitchison's book, *The Seeds of Speech* (Cambridge: Cambridge University Press, 1996, pp. 116–17).

Some studies of uptalk or high rising terminals include 'An intonation change in progress in Australian English' by Gregory Guy et al., in *Language in Society* 15 (1986), pp. 23–52, 'Linguistic change and intonation: the use of high rising terminals in New Zealand English' by David Britain, in *Language Variation and Change* 4 (1992), pp. 77–104 and 'The interpretation of the high-rise question contour in English' by Julia Hirschberg and Gregory Ward, in *Journal of Pragmatics* 24 (1995), pp. 407–12.

My study of *dove* replacing *dived* is reported with several other current changes in 'Sociolinguistic coherence of changes in a standard dialect', in *Papers from NWAVE XXV* (Philadelphia: University of Pennsylvania Press, 1996). The study of *dived* and *dove* in Texas is by Cynthia Bernstein in 'Drug usage among high-school students in Silsbee, Texas' (in *Centennial Usage Studies*, G. D. Little and M. Montgomery (ed.), Tuscaloosa: University of Alabama Press, 1994, pp. 138–43).

You Shouldn't Say 'It is Me' because 'Me' is Accusative

Laurie Bauer

In order to understand the objection expressed in the title, we first have to understand the word 'accusative'. 'Accusative' is the name of a case – so we also need to understand about case. Once that has been clarified, we need to understand a little about Latin, because the objection to *It is me* is based on Latin grammar. Then we need to ask whether English grammar is like Latin grammar in the relevant ways. Finally, we need to ask why the grammar of Latin is taken to be the model of 'good' grammar by some people.

Let us begin with the notions of 'case' and 'accusative'. There are many languages (though modern English is not one of them) where nouns have endings to show the roles they play in sentences. These different endings are called 'cases'. Since we shall need to make reference to Latin later, let us consider what happens in Latin (though the notion of case in another language is discussed in Myth 19: 'Aborigines Speak a Primitive Language'). A noun like *agricola*, 'farmer', has this form if it is the subject of the verb, the person or thing performing the action of the verb (for example in *agricola laborat*, 'the farmer works'). However, a different form is used as the direct object of the verb, the person or thing undergoing the action of the verb (for example, *puella agricolam monet*, 'the girl warns the farmer,' literally 'girl farmer warns'). The form ending in *-a* is called the nominative form of these nouns. The form ending in *-am* is called the accusative form. The English names of these cases are borrowed from the Latin. These are just two of the six case forms that nouns have in Latin, but we needn't worry about the vocative, genitive, dative or ablative cases here.

Not only nouns in Latin have case endings, but adjectives (which we need not worry about here) and pronouns, too. So if you wanted to say 'the goddess warns her' (meaning 'the girl'), for example, you would say *dea illam monet* (literally 'goddess [nominative] that-one [accusative] warns'). 'She warns the farmer,' by contrast, would be *illa agricolam monet* (literally 'that-one [nominative] the farmer [accusative] warns'). The main function of the nominative case is, as has been stated, to show which noun is the subject of the verb. One of the main functions of the accusative case is to show which noun is the direct object of the verb. The cases in a language like Latin are far more important in showing this than the order of the words, so that *dea puellam monet* and *puellam dea monet* and even *puellam monet dea* all mean 'the goddess warns the girl.' The cases show the function of the nouns, independent of their position. This is different from English where *the goddess warns the girl* and *the girl warns the goddess* mean different things. In English, where there is no case marking for ordinary nouns, the position in the sentence shows the function, and so the position is fixed.

Although showing what is subject and what is object are two of the main functions of the nominative and accusative cases in Latin, they are not the only ones. Another function of the nominative case in Latin is to mark a subject complement. A subject complement is a phrase like *the teacher* in sentences such as *Miss Smith is the teacher*. A subject complement refers to the same person as the subject of the sentence (so the teacher is the same person as Miss Smith, but in *the goddess warns the girl*, the girl is not the same person as the goddess). Subject complements occur only with a small set of verbs like *to be* (that is, the *is* in *Miss Smith is the teacher*), *to become*, and so on. So if you wanted to say, in Latin, 'Flavia is a girl,' you would say *Flavia puella est* (literally 'Flavia [nominative] girl [nominative] is').

Now let us consider whether English has nominative and accusative cases. It has been stated above that English nouns do not have case endings. But English pronouns show a system similar to that in Latin. In English you say *I warn him* but *he warns me*, using *I* and *he* as the subject of the verb and *me* and *him* as the direct object of the verb. We might, therefore, conclude that *I, he, she, we, they* are nominative case pronouns, and *me, him, her, us, them* are accusative case. *It* and *you* can be either.

If English works in just the same way as Latin, then we would expect to find *It is I* and not *It is me*. So how do pronouns in subject complements really work in English? In the King James Bible (for instance in Matthew 14:27, Mark 6:50, John 6:20) we find *It is I*, with the pronoun *I* in the subject complement, just as in Latin. However, we need to bear in mind that the King James Bible was written in English that was rather old-fashioned at the time (1611). In Shakespeare's *Twelfth Night* (II.v) Sir Andrew Aguecheek uses both *me* and *I* in this context within two lines:

MALVOLIO: *You waste the treasure of your time with a foolish knight –*
SIR ANDREW: *That's me, I warrant you.*
MALVOLIO: *One Sir Andrew.*
SIR ANDREW: *I knew 'twas I, for many do call me fool.*

The construction *It is me* was well established by this time and has been gradually gaining at the expense of *It is I* ever since. *It is me/him/her* can be found in the works of great writers of English such as Christopher Marlowe, Daniel Defoe, Jane Austen, Charlotte Brontë, Charles Dickens and Aldous Huxley, to name but a few.

Ironically, perhaps, Latin did not use the equivalent of either *It is I* or *It is me* in contexts like this. When the Latin playwright Plautus has one of his characters ask 'Who is at the gates?', the answer comes back *Ego sum* ('I am'). In English until the fifteenth century, a construction with *I am* would also have been used. The construction was usually *I am it* (though not necessarily with the words in that order). The same construction is still used in modern German: *Ich bin es* (literally 'I am it'). It would take us far beyond this chapter to try to explain why such a change should have taken place, but it did. By Shakespeare's time *It is me* was frequently heard, even if it is not the majority form in the plays of Shakespeare, Jonson and Marlowe. By the eighteenth century this construction was common enough for some grammarians to feel it was worth trying to discourage it. They pointed to the (supposed) Latin pattern and demanded *It is I*. Partly as a result of this, both constructions survive today, *It is I* having a distinctly formal ring to it. Consequently, it is used especially by those who are very conscious of their language use.

If a particular case is used in a construction in Latin, does it follow that the same case must be used in the parallel construction in English? More generally, does the structure of English (or of any language) have to be the same as the structure of Latin? The answer is very clearly 'no'.

If you look back at the examples of Latin sentences given above, you will see that *puella*, for instance, is translated as 'the girl'. But there is no word in Latin corresponding to English 'the'. No one has ever suggested that English should follow Latin in this respect and omit every occurrence of the word *the*. English does not follow Latin in that grammatical pattern and need not in others. Or consider what happens in French. The French equivalent of *it is me* is *c'est moi* (literally 'that is me'), and it would be totally impossible to say *c'est je* (literally 'that is I'), because *je* can occur only as a subject in French. Not even the French Académie has suggested that French speakers should say *c'est je*, even though French derives directly from Latin in a way that English does not. French does not follow Latin in this particular grammatical pattern. Why should English be expected to follow the Latin pattern when French does not? Why don't we say of English that *I* can only occur as a subject, as they do in French?

More generally, it is not true that all languages have the same set of grammatical constructions or patterns. It is true that there are probably no languages without nouns and verbs, no languages (except sign languages) without consonants and vowels, no languages which do not have verbs with direct objects. But the number of such absolute language universals is relatively small. While there are some languages (such as Latin and Zulu) where verbs have to be marked to show what their subject is, there are others (such as Danish and Mandarin) where there is no such marking. While there are some languages (like Latin and English) which force you to state whether a male or a female person is involved when you use a singular third-person pronoun (i.e. *he* or *she*), there are others (for instance, Finnish and Maori) which have no such requirements. Matters such as what case will be used for a particular function are very definitely in the variable class and not in the universal class.

Despite that, it is quite clear that people's view of what English should do has been strongly influenced by what Latin does. For instance, there is (or used to be – it is very infrequently observed in natural speech today) a feeling that an infinitive in English should not be split. What this means is that you should not put anything between the *to* which marks an infinitive verb and the verb itself: you should say *to go boldly* and never *to boldly go*. This 'rule' is based on Latin, where the marker of the infinitive is an ending, and you can no more split it from the rest of the verb than you can split *-ing* from the rest of its verb and say *goboldlying* for *going boldly*. English speakers clearly do not feel that *to* and *go* belong together as closely as *go* and *-ing*. They frequently put words between this kind of *to* and its verb.

Why should the patterns of Latin dictate what is acceptable in English? The reason is to be found in the role Latin played in the history of Western Europe. Latin was the language of the powerful and the learned in Western Europe for a thousand years. In Italy, Dante wrote a piece *c.* 1300 praising the use of Italian rather than Latin. He wrote it in Latin. In France a royal decree of 1539 prescribed the use of French rather than Latin in the courts of law. Erasmus, a Dutchman who died in 1536, wrote entirely in Latin. English did not become the language of the law in England until the seventeenth century.

Against this background, Latin was seen as the language of refinement and education into the eighteenth century. The prestige accorded to the churchmen, lawyers and scholars who used Latin was transferred to the language itself. Latin was held to be noble and beautiful, not just the thoughts expressed in it or the people who used it. What is called 'beauty' in a language is more accurately seen as a reflection of the prestige of its speakers. For parallel comments, see Myth 4: French is a Logical Language.

Because Latin had this prestige, people thought that English would gain similar prestige by following the patterns of the language which already had prestige. From a more detached point of view, we can say that this is making a mistake about the source of Latin's prestige.

Latin gained its prestige not from the grammatical patterns it used but from the speakers who used the language and the uses to which it was put. The Australian aboriginal language Dyirbal shares many of the linguistic features of Latin, but does not have the same social prestige because its speakers do not have powerful positions and the language is not used for highly respected functions in our society. If Dyirbal speakers had sailed around the world and colonized Great Britain and held governmental power in Britain, then Dyirbal might have high prestige – but because of its use, not its structures.

To sum up, Latin has (or had; its prestige is waning as fewer educated people use it) high prestige because of the way it was used for such a long period of time. Some people think that English would be improved if it followed the patterns of this high-prestige language more closely. One such pattern is the use of the nominative as the case of the subject complement. These people think that English is in some sense 'better' if it follows Latin grammatical rules about subject complements, and this involves saying *It is I* rather than the usual modern English pattern (and the usual pattern of a number of other languages of Western Europe) of *It is me*. To the extent that such people's opinions mold actual usage, this has now become something of a self-fulfilling prophecy.

But there is another school of thought which says that there is no real point in avoiding the normal English pattern. People who adhere to this view – and I am one of them – believe that even if languages sometimes borrow patterns from each other voluntarily, you cannot and should not impose the patterns of one language on another. To do so is like trying to make people play tennis with a golf club – it takes one set of rules and imposes them in the wrong context. It also follows that you should not impose patterns from older versions of the same language as people do when they try to insist on *whom* in *Whom did you see?* And if anyone asks who told you that, you can tell them: it was me.

Sources and further reading

For a discussion of the various constructions, examples of their use and comments on them, see F. Th. Visser, *An Historical Syntax of the English Language*, Volume I (Leiden: Brill, 1963, pp. 236–45).

They Speak Really Bad English Down South and in New York City ·

Dennis R. Preston

Imagine this. You have persistent bad headaches. Aspirin and other miracle products don't make them go away. Your family doctor decides it's time to have a specialist's opinion. He hasn't said the words, but you turn the terrible possibility over in your mind – 'Brain tumor!'

You appear at the New York City office of Dr N. V. Cramden, Brain Surgeon; you sign in and await the beginning of the process that will reveal your fate. Cramden approaches and speaks:

'Hey, how's it goin'? Rotten break, huh? Ya got a pain in da noggin'.
Don't sweat it; I'm gonna fix ya up. Hey, nois! Ovuh heah! Bring me
dat whatchamacallit. How da hell am I gonna take care of my patient
heah if you don't hand me dem tools? Dat's a goil.'

You still have your clothes on (it's a brain surgeon's office, right?), so you just head for the door, stopping at the front desk and tell the receptionist that someone in the examining room is posing as Dr Cramden. Maybe you never return to your trusted family doctor, since he or she has sent you to a quack. Whatever your decision, you do not continue under the care of Dr Cramden.

Linguists know that language variety does not correlate with intelligence or competence, so Dr Cramden could well be one of the best brain surgeons in town. Nevertheless, popular associations of certain varieties of English with professional and intellectual competence run so deep that Dr Cramden will not get to crack many crania unless he learns to sound very different.

A primary linguistic myth, one nearly universally attached to minorities, rural people and the less well educated, extends in the United States even to well-educated speakers of some regional varieties. That myth, of course, is that some varieties of a language are not as good as others.

Professional linguists are happy with the idea that some varieties of a language are more standard than others; that is a product of social facts. Higher-status groups impose their behaviors (including language) on others, claiming theirs are the standard ones. Whether you approve of that or not, the standard variety is selected through purely social processes and has not one whit more logic, historical consistency, communicative expressivity or internal complexity or systematicity than any other variety. Since every region has its own social stratification, every area also has a share of both standard and nonstandard speakers.

I admit to a little cheating above. I made Dr Cramden a little more of a tough kid from the streets than I should have. The truth is, I need not have done so. Although linguists believe that every region has its own standard variety, there is widespread belief in the US that some regional varieties are more standard than others and, indeed, that some regional varieties are far from the standard – particularly those of the South and New York City (NYC).

Please understand the intensity of this myth, for it is not a weakly expressed preference; in the US it runs deep, strong and true, and evidence for it comes from what real people (not professional linguists) believe about language variety. First, consider what northern US (Michigan) speakers have to say about the South:

(Mimics Southern speech) 'As y'all know, I came up from Texas when I was about twenty-one. And I talked like this. Probably not so bad, but I talked like this; you know I said "thiyus" ["this"] and "thayut" ["that"] and all those things. And I had to learn to learn reeeal [elongated vowel] fast how to talk like a Northerner. 'Cause if I talked like this people'd think I'm the dumbest shit around.

'Because of TV, though, I think there's a kind of standard English that's evolving. And the kind of thing you hear on the TV is something

that's broadcast across the country, so most people are aware of that, but there are definite accents in the South.'

Next, consider NYC, which fares no better, even in self-evaluation, as the American sociolinguist William Labov has shown. Here are some opinions he collected in the mid 1960s:

'I'll tell you, you see, my son is always correcting me. He speaks very well – the one that went to [two years of] college. And I'm glad that he corrects me – because it shows me that there are many times when I don't pronounce my words correctly.'

'Bill's college alumni group – we have a party once a month in Philadelphia. Well, now I know them about two years and every time we're there – at a wedding, at a party, a shower – they say, if someone new is in the group: "Listen to Jo Ann talk!" I sit there and I babble on, and they say, "Doesn't she have a ridiculous accent!" and "It's so New Yorkerish and all!" '

Such anecdotal evidence could fill many pages and includes even outsider imitations of the varieties, such as mock partings for Southerners – 'Y'all come back and see us sometime now, ya heah?' – and the following putative NYC poem which plays on the substitution of t- and d-like for th-sounds and the loss of the r-sound (and modification of the vowel) in such words as 'bird':

> *T'ree little boids sittin' on a coib,*
> *Eatin' doity woims and sayin' doity woids.*

These informal assessments are bolstered by quantitative studies. Nearly 150 people from south-eastern Michigan (of European-American ethnicity, of both sexes and of all ages and social classes) rated (on a scale of one to ten) the degree of 'correctness' of English spoken in the fifty states, Washington, DC, and NYC. Figure 1 shows the average scores for this task.

These responses immediately confirm what every American knows

– the lowest ratings are for the South and NYC (and nearby New Jersey, infected by its proximity to the NYC metropolitan area). Only these areas score averages below '5'; Alabama, the heart of the horrible South, scores in the '3' range.

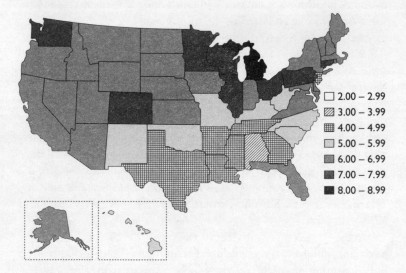

Figure 1: Mean scores of the rankings for 'correct English' of the fifty states, Washington, DC, and NYC by south-eastern Michigan respondents ('1' = 'worst English'; '10' = 'best English')

Although it is not the major focus here, it is also clear that the Michiganders doing these ratings think pretty well of themselves; they give their home state a ranking in the '8' range, the only area so rewarded. Linguists call such local hubris 'linguistic security'. It is not hard to determine why: Michiganders believe another interesting myth – that they do not speak a dialect at all (although, as any linguist will assert, if you speak a human language, you must speak some dialect of it, even if it is a bland Michigan one). When Michigan respondents carry out another task, which asks them to draw on a blank map of the US where they think the various dialect areas are and label them, results such as Figure 2 emerge, confirming their local linguistic pride.

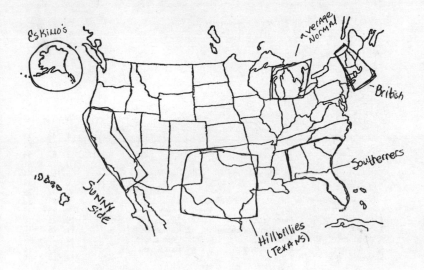

Figure 2: Hand-drawn map of a Michigan respondent's idea of the dialect areas of the US

The respondent who drew Figure 2 places only Michigan in the 'normal' area and, as we would expect from the rankings of Figure 1, impolite things are said about the South (although not NYC). If one studies a large number of such hand-drawn maps, it is possible to produce a generalized map such as Figure 3. This map shows not only where Michigan respondents draw lines for the areas of the US but also how many respondents drew a boundary around each one. The most important thing to note about Figure 3 is the number of Michigan respondents who drew a South – 138 out of 147 (94 per cent). Even the home area (which houses the uniquely correct Michigan speech) is registered as a separate speech region by only 90 respondents (61 per cent). The third most frequently drawn area is, not surprisingly, the area which contains NYC (80; 54 per cent).

These Michiganders seem, therefore, to hear dialect differences not as linguists do – on the basis of objective differences in the language system – but on the basis of their evaluation of the correctness of

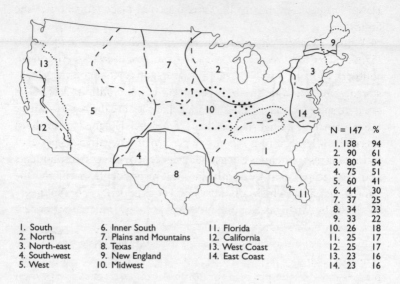

			N = 147	%
			1. 138	94
			2. 90	61
			3. 80	54
			4. 75	51
			5. 60	41
			6. 44	30
			7. 37	25
			8. 34	23
			9. 33	22
1. South	6. Inner South	11. Florida	10. 26	18
2. North	7. Plains and Mountains	12. California	11. 25	17
3. North-east	8. Texas	13. West Coast	12. 25	17
4. South-west	9. New England	14. East Coast	13. 23	16
5. West	10. Midwest		14. 23	16

Figure 3: Generalized map of 147 Michigan respondents' idea of the dialect areas of the US

areas. The linguistic South, the area perceived most consistently as incorrect, quite simply exists for these respondents more than any other area.

Michiganders are not unique; in other areas where this work has been done, a South is always drawn by the highest percentage of respondents – South Carolina 94 per cent, NYC 92 per cent, western New York 100 per cent, southern Indiana 86 per cent and Oregon 92 per cent. Only Hawai'ians recognize another area (their own) more frequently, and only marginally (97 per cent Hawai'i; 94 per cent South).

Also important to these respondents is the other place where they believe bad English is spoken. A 'North-east' (a small area with a focus in NYC) or NYC itself figures very high in the percentages – South Carolina 46 per cent, NYC itself 64 per cent, western New York 45 per cent, southern Indiana 51 per cent, Oregon 75 per cent and

Hawai'i 57 per cent, nearly all of these second-place scores (after the South).

A study of labels on hand-drawn maps, such as the one shown in Figure 2, by fifty respondents each from south-eastern Michigan, southern Indiana, South Carolina and Oregon further confirms these stereotypes. The intensity of recognition of the South and NYC as separate speech areas parallels the idea that they are the regions where the most incorrect English is spoken. Of the labels assigned to Southern speech by Michigan respondents 22 per cent are negative; 36 per cent by Indiana respondents are negative; 31 per cent by Oregon respondents and even 20 per cent by South Carolina respondents. Similarly, the 'North-east' area (which contains NYC) fares poorly: 15 per cent negative labels by Michigan respondents; 18 per cent by Indiana; 24 per cent by Oregon and a whopping 65 per cent by South Carolina.

Negative labels assigned to speech areas overall were low (13 per cent for Michigan respondents; 22 per cent for Indiana, 18 per cent for Oregon – but 32 per cent for South Carolina, a reflection of their evaluation of much non-Southern territory for the entire US, e.g. 33 per cent for California and 30 per cent for the Midwest). One South Carolina respondent identifies everything north of the Mason-Dixon line with the notation 'Them – The Bad Guys' in contrast to the label for the entire South: 'Us – The Good Guys'. Other Southerners note that Northern speech is 'mean' or 'rude', and one calls it 'scratch and claw'. A common caricature of NYC speech refers to its 'nasal' quality and its rate (fast).

There are labels for Southerners, like 'Hillbillies' and 'Hicks', but there are far more 'linguistic' designations – 'drawl', 'twang', 'Rebel slang', and many references to speed (slow).

Finally, what about a quantitative analysis of Southerners' views of the correctness issue? Figure 4 shows the ratings by thirty-six Auburn University students (principally from Alabama, a few from Georgia, and South Carolina).

NYC fares even worse here than in the Michigan ratings; it is the only area to fall in the '3' range. Antipathy to NYC from the South is obvious. Other ratings for correctness, however, show none of the

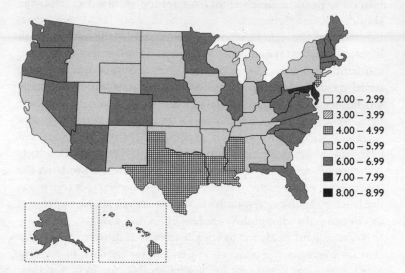

Figure 4: Mean scores of the rankings of the fifty states, Washington, DC, and NYC for 'correct English' by Auburn University (Alabama) students (ratings as in Figure 1)

strength and certainty of the Michigan opinions seen in Figure 1. Michigan respondents consider their speech the best and steadily assign lower ratings the farther South a state is. Imagine a Michigander's disdain for an evaluation of correct English which, as Figure 4 shows, rates the territory from Michigan to Alabama as an undifferentiated '5'!

These 'eastern' Southern respondents, however, also find parts of the South especially lacking in correct English, namely the Mississippi, Louisiana and Texas areas just to the west of them, which they put in the '4' range. Their own areas (rated in the '5' and '6' ranges) are neither fish nor fowl, and they reserve the best ratings (only one step up at '7') for Maryland and the national capital, Washington, DC, both areas within a more general southern speech region.

Southerners pretty clearly suffer from what linguists would call 'linguistic insecurity', but they manage to deflect the disdain of Northerners to adjacent areas rather than suffer the principal shame locally. They do not rate themselves at the top of the heap (as Michiganders do), and they appear to associate 'correct English' with some official or national status (Washington, DC).

If Southerners don't find their own speech correct, can they find anything redeeming about it? Figure 5 shows what these same Southerners believe about language 'pleasantness'.

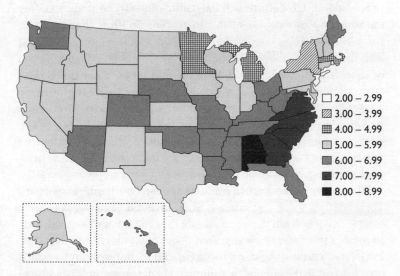

2.00 – 2.99
3.00 – 3.99
4.00 – 4.99
5.00 – 5.99
6.00 – 6.99
7.00 – 7.99
8.00 – 8.99

Figure 5: Mean scores of the rankings for 'pleasant English' by Auburn University (Alabama) students ('1' = 'least pleasant English'; '10' = 'most pleasant English')

Here is the neat reversal of Figure 1 which did not emerge in Figure 4. Just as Michiganders found their variety 'most correct' ('8'), these principally Alabama students find theirs 'most pleasant' (also '8'). As one moves north, a steady disapproval of the 'friendly' aspects of speech (what linguists like to call the 'solidarity' aspects) emerges, leaving Michigan part of a pretty unhospitable northern area, itself a '4'.

There is one thing, however, that Michiganders and Alabamians agree on. NYC (and its partner in linguistic 'grime', nearby New

Jersey) are at the bottom of the scale for both 'correctness' and 'pleasantness'. (In fact, the '2' in Figure 5 for New Jersey is the lowest average rating for any area ever assigned in these tests.)

In summary, respondents from all over the US confirm the myth that some regions speak better English than others, and they do not hesitate to indicate that NYC and the South are on the bottom of that pile.

Students of US culture will have little difficulty in understanding the sources of the details of this myth. The South is thought to be rural, backward and uneducated; its dialect is quite simply associated with the features assigned its residents. NYC fares little better. As one of Labov's respondents told him in the mid 1960s, 'They think we're all murderers.' Just as US popular culture has kept alive the barefoot, moonshine-making and drinking, intermarrying, racist Southerner, so has it continued to contribute to the perception of the brash, boorish, criminal, violent New Yorker. Small wonder that the varieties of English associated with these areas have these characteristics attributed to them.

Like all groups who are prejudiced against, Southerners (and New Yorkers) fight back by making their despised language variety a solidarity symbol, but there is no doubt they suffer linguistic insecurity in spite of this defensive maneuver.

Since you now understand that a belief in the superiority or inferiority of regional varieties is simply a US language myth, you can apologetically approach your good old family doctor about the headache problem again. Of course, you are too embarrassed to return to Cramden's office, so you ask for another referral and are sent to Dr B. J. ('Jimmy') Peaseblossom. You are relieved to hear his dulcet tones as he approaches:

'Bubba, haw's it hangin'? Cain't buy no luck, kin yuh? Yore hay-ud ailin' yuh? Don't git all flustrated; I'm gonna fix yew up good. Sweetheart! Looka hyeah! Bring me that thayngamabob, wouldja? How kin Ah take keer of ol' Bubba without mah thayngs? Thank yuh honey!'

Your headaches turn out to be hangovers.

Sources and further reading

The maps and data are taken from my collections. Readers who want an introduction to the folk perceptions of regional speech in the United States may consult my *Perceptual Dialectology* (Dordrecht: Foris, 1989). A current survey of recent and earlier work in this area (including research from the Netherlands, Japan, Germany, Wales, Turkey and France) appears under my editorship as *A Handbook of Perceptual Dialectology* (Beverly Hills, CA: Sage, 1997). The quotations from New Yorkers are taken from William Labov's seminal work on NYC speech, *The Social Stratification of English in New York City* (Arlington, VA: The Center for Applied Linguistics, 1966). The work on Oregon has been carried out by Laura Hartley and is reported in *Oregonian Perceptions of American Regional Speech* (East Lansing, MI: MA thesis, Department of Linguistics and Languages, Michigan State University, 1996).

A quantitative method for calculating linguistic insecurity is first introduced in Labov's work cited above but refined and extended to gender in Peter Trudgill's 'Sex, covert prestige and linguistic change in the urban British English of Norwich' in *Language in Society* 1 (1972), pp. 179–95. A good introduction to the techniques and principal findings of the study of language attitudes (and to the functions of language for 'status' and 'solidarity') may be found in Ellen Bouchard Ryan and Howard Giles (eds.), *Attitudes Towards Language Variation* (London: Arnold, 1982).

Some Languages are Spoken More Quickly than Others

Peter Roach

We all make judgements about how quickly someone is speaking, but it is not at all easy to work out what we base these judgements on. Speakers of some languages seem to rattle away at high speed like machine-guns, while other languages sound rather slow and plodding. We find the same when we listen to dialects of our own native language – within English, for example, it is a familiar cliché that cowboys in Westerns (usually set in Texas or neighbouring states) speak slowly, with a drawl. English rural accents of East Anglia and the South-West are also thought of as slow-speaking, while urban accents such as those of London or New York are more often thought of as fast-speaking. However, impressionistic judgements about such things are often unreliable. Ilse Lehiste, who has studied very many languages, wrote, 'Whether there are differences in the rates of speech of speakers with different linguistic backgrounds is not well known' (Lehiste, p. 52). More recently, Laver has written, 'The analysis of phenomena such as rate is dangerously open to subjective bias . . . listeners' judgements rapidly begin to lose objectivity when the utterance concerned comes either from an unfamiliar accent or (even worse) from an unfamiliar language' (p. 542). Can we establish scientifically that there really are characteristic differences in speaking speed? There are, it seems to me, three possibilities:

(1) some languages really are spoken more rapidly, and some more slowly, than others as a natural result of the way their sounds are produced.

(2) we get the impression that some languages are spoken more quickly than others because of some sort of illusion.

(3) in some societies it is socially acceptable or approved to speak rapidly, and in others slow speaking is preferred.

1. Measures of speaking in different languages

We need to look for appropriate ways to measure how quickly someone is talking. We are used to measuring the speed at which someone can type, write or take shorthand dictation in terms of how many words per minute are taken down. Some adjustment usually has to be made to penalize someone for going so quickly that they make a lot of mistakes. In measuring speech, we can do the same thing – we can give someone a passage to read, or a speaking task such as describing what they did on their last holiday, and count how many words they speak in a given time. However, in speech it makes a big difference whether or not we include pauses. If I want to work out how long it took me to cycle somewhere, I might make a note of my times both including and excluding rest stops that I made on the way. In a similar way, most studies of speaking have found it necessary to make two different measurements of the rate at which we produce units of speech: the rate including pauses and hesitations, and the rate excluding such things. The terms usually used are *speaking rate* and *articulation rate* (Laver). Both are highly correlated with perceived speech tempo, according to van Bezooyen. Tauroza and Allison measured words per minute, syllables per minute and syllables per word in different styles of spoken English and found substantial differences. It is quite possible that some languages make more use of pauses and hesitations than others, and our perception of speed of speaking could be influenced by this (Ofuka). In comparing different languages, however, there is a more serious problem: some languages (e.g. German, Hungarian) have some very long words, while others (e.g. Chinese) have very few words of more than one or two syllables. It has been found that Finnish is faster than English if syllables per second are measured, but slower if words are counted, since Finnish words tend to be longer than English words. Much depends, of course, on how we define what a word is (Palmer, pp. 41–8). This inter-language difference could have a serious impact on the accuracy of our measurements, and for this reason many investigators have chosen instead to measure the number of *syllables* spoken in a given amount of time. This usually results in a syllables-per-second measurement, and at this more detailed level of measurement it is usual to exclude pauses. This is not the end to our problems, however: although counting syllables is likely to be a much more reliable way of comparing different languages for speaking rate than counting words, we should bear in mind that different languages have very different syllable structures. Many of the world's languages do not use syllables with more than three or four sounds, while others allow syllables of many more sounds. In English, for example, the word 'strengths' /streŋθs/ contains seven sounds; the six-syllable English sentence 'Smith's strength crunched twelve strong trucks' (containing thirty-two sounds) would take much longer to say than the six-syllable Japanese phrase 'kakashi to risu' which contains twelve sounds. So if a language with a relatively simple syllable structure like Japanese is able to fit more syllables into a second than a language with a complex syllable structures such as English or Polish, it will probably sound faster as a result. Dauer (personal communication) has found that Greek and Italian are spoken more rapidly than English in terms of syllables per second, but this difference disappears when sounds per second are counted. It seems, then, that we should compare languages' speaking rates by measuring the number of *sounds* produced per second, rather than the number of syllables. Within a particular language, it is clear that speech rate as measured in sounds per second does vary quite widely: Fonagy and Magdics measured different speaking styles and found rates varying from 9.4 sounds (average) per second for poetry reading to 13.83 per second for sports commentary. But this still leaves us with a problem. The faster we speak, the more sounds we leave out. Speaking slowly, I might pronounce the sentence 'She looked particularly interesting' as /ʃi lukt pətɪkjələli ɪntərəstɪŋ/, which contains twenty-seven sounds but, speaking rapidly, I might say /ʃi luk pətɪkli ɪntrstɪŋ/, which contains only twenty sounds. In theory, then, it could happen that in speaking quickly I might produce no more sounds per second than when speaking slowly. In order to get a meaningful measure it would be necessary to count not the sounds actually observable in the physical signal, but the 'underlying phonemes' that I would have produced in careful speech. Osser and Peng measured sounds per second for speakers of Japanese and of American English and found no significant difference between them. Den Os compared Dutch and Italian and found no significant difference in terms of syllables per second, though Italian was somewhat slower in terms of sounds per second. In a review of measurements of a number of different languages, Dankovicova quotes average figures from various studies: for German, 5.55 and 5.7 syllables per second, for French 5.29, 5.2 and 5.7 syl/sec, for Dutch 6.1 and for Italian 6.4. These are all for 'normal' speaking rate – in different circumstances, of course, rates can vary. I have a recording of a friend who left a message on my telephone answering machine and kept up an average speed of over 8 syl/sec over a period of about 20 seconds. Arnfield and Roach showed rates in English varying between 3.3 and 5.9 syl/sec. But, overall, it seems that on the evidence available at present, there is no real difference between different languages in terms of sounds per second in normal speaking cycles.

How might we pursue this question further? One possibility would be to make use of some of the carefully assembled speech databases stored on computer which have been phonetically labelled. Databases such as EUROM-1 (Chan), which comprises speech of six Western European languages and BABEL (Roach et al.) containing five languages of Eastern Europe, will, when complete and available to researchers, give us valuable new material. But the expectation is that these collections of normal, unemotional monologues will give us the same answers as the other surveys – we will find no difference between languages in terms of sounds per second or syllables per second.

2. Speaking rate as an illusion

Our impression of a language being spoken faster or slower may depend to some extent on its characteristic rhythm. More precisely, it is said that we are influenced by whether a language is perceived to be *stress-timed* or *syllable-timed*. The distinction was given a detailed exposition by Abercrombie though the idea had been proposed long before by Pike. Pike refers to the 'pattering' effect of Spanish speakers and their 'sharp-cut syllable-by-syllable pronunciation' (p. 37). Most people feel intuitively that there is a genuine rhythmical difference between languages such as English (classed as stress-timed) and French or Spanish (classed as syllable-timed), and it usually seems that syllable-timed speech sounds faster than stress-timed to speakers of stress-timed languages. So Spanish, French and Italian sound fast to English speakers, but Russian and Arabic don't. The theory suggests that in syllable-timed languages all syllables tend to be given equal amounts of time, while in stress-timed languages more time is given to stressed syllables and less to unstressed. In addition, it is said that stressed syllables occur at regular intervals of time in stress-timed languages. Unfortunately, many studies based on detailed measurement of time-intervals in different languages (e.g. Roach; Dauer) have been unable to confirm these claims, with the result that we are forced to retreat to a weaker claim: that some languages *sound* stress-timed and others *sound* syllable-timed. We may be forced to accept something similar in answer to our present question – perhaps languages and dialects just *sound* faster or slower, without any physically measurable difference. The apparent speed of some languages might simply be an illusion.

One of the questions raised by this possibility is the degree to which listeners can detect differences of speaking rate in their own language and in other languages. If it turns out that we are no good at detecting speed differences in different languages, we will have to conclude that our judgements of speaking rate are unreliable. Vaane carried out a study using recordings of Dutch (the subjects' native language), English, French, Spanish and Moroccan Arabic; these were spoken at three different rates. Two groups of listeners, one phonetically trained and the other untrained, had to try to judge the speed of utterance. Vaane tested the hypothesis that we will be less adept at judging the speed of a language we do not know, and an unknown language is likely to sound faster than our own language (presumably because it 'sounds harder to do'). Her results suggest that in fact both trained and untrained listeners are quite accurate in judging the rate of speaking for their own language and also for languages with which they are unfamiliar, a finding which compares interestingly with the view quoted from Laver above. From this we can conclude that the judgements are not based on linguistic knowledge (such as we use in identifying words). We must be using one or more detectable phonetic characteristics of the speech whether or not we know the language being spoken.

Useful though the above findings are, they do not yet bring us an answer to the question of whether some languages are spoken more rapidly than others (when situational and personal factors have been taken into account). Vaane does quote mean syllables-per-second rates for the test passages in her experiment, but does not tell us if the inter-language differences are statistically significant. Interestingly, Dutch comes out with the highest speaking rate in all three conditions, though this is not a language that most English people would immediately think of as being rapidly spoken.

3. Social and personal factors and speaking rate

Social factors influence the speakers of a language in different ways: a number of anecdotal sources suggest that in some societies it is regarded as acceptable or approved to speak rapidly, while in others slow speech is preferred. There is almost certainly an interaction with gender here, with slow speech usually being preferred for males. This would mean that, while *at normal speaking speed* the sounds-per-second rate for all languages may be effectively the same, some languages are characteristically using higher and lower speaking rates than other languages in particular social situations. In a carefully controlled study, Kowal et al. looked at two very different types of speech (story-telling and taking part in interviews) in English, Finnish, French, German and Spanish. They found significant differences between the two styles of speech (both in terms of the amount of pausing and of the speaking rate) but no significant difference between the languages. They concluded that the influence of the language is negligible compared with the influence of the style of speech. Similarly, Barik showed that differences in tempo between English and French were due to the style of speech, not to the language. Certainly we are all capable of speaking faster and slower when we want to. There are variations in speed associated with the situation in which the speech is being produced – we speak more rapidly if we are in a hurry, or saying something urgent, or trying not to be interrupted in a conversation. We tend to speak more slowly when we are tired or bored. The emotional state of the speaker at the time of speaking is clearly influential. There seems also to be a personal factor – some people are naturally fast talkers, while others habitually speak slowly, within the same language and dialect and in the same situation. Research has shown that our opinion of speakers is influenced by their speaking rate: Giles reports that 'a positive linear relationship has repeatedly been found between speech rate and perceived competence,' and Stephen Cowley (personal communication) says that in Zulu society, slow speech tempo is a sign of respect and sincerity. Yet another social factor is the amount of temporal variability, where the alternation between speaking rapidly and speaking slowly may itself have considerable communicative value – this has been pointed out by Cowley, who has found very wide tempo variation from phrase to phrase among Italian speakers in conversational data.

While this idea of social determination of speed seems the most plausible explanation, the only way we are going to be able to test it is by much more research across a wide variety of languages and social situations. Let us hope that this research will be carried out.

My thanks to Bill Barry, Stephen Cowley, Jana Dankovicova and Marianne Jessen for their advice and discussion.

Sources and further reading

Abercrombie, D., *Elements of General Phonetics*, Edinburgh: Edinburgh University Press, 1967.
Arnfield, S., Roach, P., Setter, J., Greasley, P. and Horton, D.,

'Emotional stress and speech tempo variation', *Proceedings of the ESCA/NATO Workshop on Speech Under Stress*, Lisbon, 1995, pp. 13–15.

Barik, H. C., 'Cross-linguistic study of temporal characteristics of different types of speech materials', *Language and Speech*, 20, 1977, pp. 116–26.

Bezooyen, R. van, *Characteristics and Recognizability of Vocal Expressions of Emotion*, Dordrecht: Foris, 1984.

Chan, D. and others, 'EUROM: A spoken language resource for the EU', in *Proceedings of Eurospeech 95*, Madrid, 1995, pp. 867–70.

Cowley, S., 'Conversational functions of rhythmical patterning', *Language and Communication*, vol. 14.4, 1994, pp. 353–76.

Dankovicova, J., 'Variability in articulation rate in spontaneous Czech speech', unpublished M.Phil. thesis, University of Oxford, 1994.

Dauer, 'Stress-timing and syllable-timing re-analysed', *Journal of Phonetics*, vol. 11, 1983, pp. 51–62.

Den Os, E. A., *Rhythm and Tempo of Dutch and Italian*, Utrecht: Drukkerij Elinkwijk, 1988.

Fonagy, I. and Magdics, K., 'Speed of utterance in phrases of different lengths, *Language and Speech*, 4, 1960, pp. 179–92.

Giles, H., 'Speech tempo', in W. Bright (ed.), *The Oxford International Encyclopedia of Linguistics*. Oxford: Oxford University Press, 1992.

Kowal, S., Wiese, R. and O'Connell, D., 'The use of time in storytelling', *Language and Speech*, vol. 26.4, 1983, pp. 377–92.

Laver, J., *Principles of Phonetics*, Cambridge: Cambridge University Press, 1995.

Lehiste, I., *Suprasegmentals*, MA: MIT Press, 1970.

Ofuka, E., *Acoustic and Perceptual Analyses of Politeness in Japanese Speech*, unpublished Ph.D. thesis, Leeds: University of Leeds, 1996.

Osser, H. and Peng, F., 'A cross-cultural study of speech rate', *Language and Speech*, 7, 1964, pp. 120–5.

Palmer, F. R., *Grammar*, Harmondsworth: Penguin, 1984 (2nd edn).

Pike, K. L., *The Intonation of American English*, East Lansing: University of Michigan Press, 1945.

Roach, P., 'On the distinction between "stress-timed" and "syllable-timed" languages', in D. Crystal (ed.), *Linguistic Controversies*, London: Edward Arnold, 1982.

Roach, P., Arnfield, S. and Hallum, E., 'BABEL: A multi-language database', *Proceedings of the Australian International Conference on Speech Science and Technology* (SST-96), pp. 351–4.

Tauroza, S. and Allison, D., 'Speech rates in British English', *Applied Linguistics*, 11, 1990, pp. 90–115.

Vaane, E., 'Subjective estimation of speech rate', *Phonetica*, vol. 39, 1982, pp. 136–49.

MYTH 19

Aborigines Speak a Primitive Language

Nicholas Evans

As a linguist who spends much time researching Australian Aboriginal languages, I have often been informed by people I have met in my travels that 'You must have an easy job – it must be pretty simple figuring out the grammar of such a primitive language.' If you go further and ask your travelling companions over a beer or six why they hold this belief, you encounter a number of sub-myths:

There is just one Aboriginal language.
Aboriginal languages have no grammar.
The vocabularies of Aboriginal languages are simple and lack
    detail; alternatively, they are cluttered with details and
    unable to deal with abstractions.
Aboriginal languages may be all right in the bush, but they
    can't deal with the twentieth century.

I'll deal with each of these individually below. Two of these myths are dealt with elsewhere in this book, and I shall deal with those in rather less detail.

So, you can speak Aborigine?

The first white arrivals in Botany Bay came equipped with an Aboriginal vocabulary recorded by Captain Cook and others in Cooktown, north Queensland but soon found this was of no more use in communicating with the owners of the Botany Bay region than a Lithuanian phrasebook would be in London: Captain Cook recorded the Guugu

Yimidhirr language (giving us the word *kangaroo* in the process), while the language of the Sydney region was Dhaaruk, only distantly related. In fact, Aboriginal Australia displays striking linguistic diversity and, traditionally, around 250 languages, further subdivisable into many dialects, were spoken over the continent. Many Aboriginal communities would prefer to count these dialects as distinct languages. If we did this, we would have to elevate this figure to about 600.

Some languages are, of course, more closely related than others. In Western Arnhem Land, for example, such languages as Mayali and Dalabon are as closely related as English and Dutch, so that 'I will eat fish' is *ngangun djenj* and *ngahnguniyan djenj* respectively. Others, such as Ilgar, are only very distantly related (more distant from Mayali and Dalabon than English is from Bengali, although Mayali and Ilgar are spoken only a couple of hundred kilometres apart), so that 'I will eat fish' in Ilgar is *anyarrun yihab*.

With so many languages spoken by a population of at most three quarters of a million, you can easily work out that the average language would only have a couple of thousand speakers. But, of course, people's social universes were much larger than this. This meant that by adulthood it was normal to be multilingual; this was made easier by the fact that most people married spouses with a different language to their own, so that children grew up speaking both the mother's and the father's languages, as well as other languages their grandparents, for example, may have spoken. For example, my Ilgar teacher, Charlie Wardaga, learned Ilgar from his father, as well as Marrgu from older people in the area he grew up in, Garig and Manangkari from other relatives, Gunwinygu from one grandparent (and he took a Gunwinygu-speaking wife and frequently sings at ceremonial gatherings where Gunwinygu is the common language) and Iwaidja through living in the Minjilang community where it is the dominant language.

There's no grammar – you can just chuck the words together in any order.

In the first difficult weeks when I was beginning to learn the Kayardild language of Bentinck Island in Queensland I experienced the usual language-learner's nightmare of failing to understand most of what was said. One of my more considerate teachers, Pluto Bentinck, would help me by repeating each sentence, working his way through all possible orderings of its words: *dangkaa bangaya kurrija, dangkaa kurrija bangaya, bangaya dangkaa kurrija, dangkaa kurrija ngada,* and so on. Given that *dangkaa* means 'the/a man', *kurrija* 'see(s)', and *bangaa* 'the/a turtle', how could he put the words in any order without changing the meaning from 'the man sees the turtle' to 'the turtle sees the man'?

Speakers of a language like Kayardild have this freedom because the identification of who does what is carried out by so-called case markers on the ends of words: the *-ya* on *bangaya* marks it as the object of the verb and hence the thing seen, while the *-a* on the end of *dangkaa* marks it as the subject and hence the seer. So while it is true that words can be put in any order, it does not indicate lack of grammar – grammar, as a code for expressing meaning, can take many forms in different languages, and here (as in Latin or Russian) the work is done by word endings rather than word ordering (see Myth 10: Some Languages Have No Grammar). You should be able to work out for yourself six ways of saying 'the turtle sees the man'; see answer 1 at the end of this chapter.

This system of case endings is so efficient that it allows parts of sentences to be specific in ways that aren't always clear in English. Consider the sentence 'The man saw the turtle on the beach.' Who is on the beach – the man, the turtle or both? Kayardild expresses each of these meanings differently – where it is the turtle on the beach, the 'associative' suffix *-nurru* is added to *ngarn-* 'beach', and the resultant *ngarnnurru* receives a further *-ya* to link it clearly to the object, giving *dangkaa bangaya kurrija ngarnnurruya* (or any other of the $4 \times 3 \times 2$ possible word orderings). If it is the man on the beach,

-nurru is used again, plus *-wa* to link it with 'man' (*a* cannot directly follow *u*, so a *w* is inserted): *dangkaa bangaya kurrija ngarrnnurruwa*, and the other orderings. And if both are on the beach, a different suffix *-ki* is used, giving *dangkaa bangaya kurrija ngarnki*, and so forth.

Not all grammars of Aboriginal languages work in the same way as Kayardild, of course – any more than English and Russian work in the same way. For example, Mayali from Western Arnhem Land is a 'polysynthetic' language that builds up highly complex verbs able to express a complete sentence, such as *ngabanmarneyawoyhwarrgah-ganjginjeng* 'I cooked the wrong meat for them again,' which can be broken down into *nga-* 'I', *ban-* 'them', *marne-* 'for', *yawoyh-* 'again', *warrgah-* 'wrongly directed action', *ganj-* 'meat', *ginje-* 'cook' and *-ng* 'past tense'.

Australian Aboriginal pronoun systems are in some ways more explicit than English as well. The main way of showing number in Dalabon from Western Arnhem Land is through the pronoun prefixed to the verb. So we find:

> *biyi* *kah-boninj*
> man he-went
> 'The man went.'

> *biyi* *barrah-boninj*
> man they two-went
> 'The two men went.'

> *biyi* *balah-boninj*
> man they-went
> 'The men went.'

But that is not all. Another way of saying 'the two men went' would be *biyi keh-boninj*. This would be appropriate if the men were related 'disharmonically' – i.e. in odd-numbered generations, like father and son, or uncle and nephew, e.g. *be ko keh-boninj* 'they two, father and son, went.' The 'harmonic' form, *barrah-boninj*, is only appropriate for people in even-numbered generations, such as brothers, spouses or grandparents with grandchildren, e.g. *winjkin-ko barrah-boninj* 'they two, grandmother and grandchild, went.'

In a short article like this we can only scratch the surface, but it should be clear by now that Aboriginal grammars have plenty to engage your analytic powers.

Just a few hundred words and you've got it all

However complicated the grammars, surely the vocabularies are pretty simple? After all, there are no words for 'neutron', 'virus' or 'terra nullius', so that's three down already. Assertions like this usually take one of two forms – either the languages are supposed to have a welter of detailed words but be incapable of generalizing, or they are just said to have very general words with too few to be precise. On both counts such submyths are wildly wrong.

The fine detail and nuanced observation of Aboriginal vocabularies is so great that I will only have space to consider a few words for the natural world, though one could make similar points with terms for emotions, or smells and fragrances, or ways of moving. Many plant and animal species had distinct names in the Aboriginal languages in whose territories they are found well before they had been recognized as species by Western taxonomic biology. The Oenpelli python, for example, has had the long-established Kunwinjku name *nawaran* but was only identified as a distinct species in the 1960s, whereupon it received the Linnean name *Morelia oenpelliensis*.

To get an idea of the degree of conciseness and detail in the biological vocabulary of a typical Aboriginal language, compare the Kunwinjku kangaroo terms with their English equivalents, in the table overleaf.

In addition to the various detailed terms just given, Kunwinjku also has a general term, *kunj*, to cover all the macropods, i.e. all kangaroos and wallabies; in English we only have the scientific term *macropod* to denote this category. And in addition to these different

Linnean and English names	Male	Female	Child
Macropus antilopinus (antilopine wallaroo)	karndakidj kalaba (large individual male)	karndayh	djamunbuk (juvenile male)
Macropus bernardus (black wallaroo)	nadjinem baark	djukerre	
Macropus robustus (wallaroo)	kalkberd kanbulerri (large male)	wolerrk	narrobad (juvenile male)
Macropus agilis (agile wallaby)	warradjangkal/ kornobolo nakurdakurda (very large individual)	merlbbe/kornobolo	nakornborrh nanjid (baby)

nouns, Kunwinjku also has different verbs to describe the different manners of hopping of these various macropods – *kamawudme* for the hopping of male antilopine wallaroo, *kadjalwahme* for the hopping of the corresponding female, *kanjedjme* for the hopping of the wallaroo, *kamurlbardme* for the hopping of the black wallaroo, and *kalurlhlurlme* for the hopping of the agile wallaby. This focus on identifying macropods by the peculiarities of their gait is particularly interesting in the light of recent work on computer vision programs able to identify wallaby species, which had far more success doing this on the basis of their movement than their static appearance.

Quite apart from finely classifying different entities, vocabularies of Aboriginal languages often also show the ecological links between particular plant and animal species. For example, the Mparntwe Arrernte language of the Alice Springs area, where various types of grub are an important source of food, has a method of naming grubs after the bushes where you can find them: *tnyeme* 'witchetty bush' yields the *tnyematye* 'witchetty grub', *utnerrenge* 'emu bush' yields the grub known as *utnerrengatye*, and you can work out for yourself the name of the grub found in *thenge*, the ironwood tree (see answers).

Sometimes there is no term in the ordinary language to cover certain more general categories, but special language varieties learned in adulthood and used under restricted circumstances possess the more abstract terms. The most extreme example of special abstract language is found on Mornington Island, where second-degree initiates, to become full men, had to learn a special initiation language known as Demiin, which had only about 200 words and hence needed to be highly abstract. For example, the complex Lardil pronoun system, where there are nineteen distinct pronouns in the ordinary language, is collapsed to two in Demiin – *n!aa* 'group containing me – i.e. I or we' and *n!uu* 'group not containing me, i.e. you, he, she, they'. (*n!* denotes a 'clicked' *n*-sound, for Demiin also has special sounds not used in the everyday language.)

They might be OK in the bush, but there's no way they can deal with the modern world

Languages tend to have the richest vocabulary in those areas in which their speakers have been interested long enough to develop specialized terms. In the early Middle Ages it was widely believed that only Latin had a sufficiently sophisticated vocabulary to discuss law, theology, medicine and science, but as various nations began to use their mother tongues more widely, each modern European language (English, French, German and so on) soon developed its own terms. Aboriginal languages are at a similar point today – they lack many terms, but their rich grammars give them the capacity to develop them when they are needed. (See also Myth 2: Some Languages are Just Not Good Enough.)

It is natural that Aboriginal languages should have developed their vocabularies most in such realms as the Australian biota and geography, kinship and so on and not in areas that have not traditionally been a central part of Aboriginal culture – such as financial transactions, nautical terminology or nuclear physics. However, just as English has responded to the encounters between its speakers and the Australian continent by coining new terms, such as the macropod terms we discussed above, so have speakers of Aboriginal languages responded by creating new terms to deal with the proliferation of novel concepts that contact with Europeans and with late-twentieth-century technology more generally, has brought.

Making up a new word from scratch is not a usual method of doing this in any language. Instead, the usual three methods are to build up new words from the existing resources of the language for compounding or affixation (e.g. *downsize* in English), to borrow words from other languages (e.g. *sputnik*) and to extend the meanings of existing words (e.g. *surfing the net*). Each of these methods has been widely employed by Aboriginal languages.

As an example of compounding, Kayardild has created the words *wadubayiinda* for 'tobacco', by compounding *wadu* 'smoke' with the root *bayii-* 'be bitten', literally 'that by means of which the smoke is bitten', and, for 'car', the word *duljawinda*, literally 'ground-runner'.

Many languages have borrowed their words for days and months, higher numbers, government institutions and Western medicine from English. Often the pronunciations of borrowed words are changed to the point where their original source is not recognizable: the English word 'hospital' ends up as *wijipitirli* in Warlpiri.

Extending existing word meanings has been a common solution to the problem of coining new vocabulary for automobiles. In Kunwinjku, for example, *kun-denge* 'foot' also means 'wheel', *kun-rakmo* 'hip' also means 'wheel housing', and the term for 'to get a flat tyre' compounds *kun-rakmo* with the verb *belngdan* 'to settle, as of mud stirred up in water' to give *rakmo-belngdanj* 'it has a flat tyre' (literally 'its hip has settled'). Combinations of compounding and extension of meaning are a common way of dealing with novel concepts – when a text on nuclear physics had to be translated into Warlpiri, for example, a new compound verb was coined to mean 'cause nuclear fission' by using a root meaning 'hit' and an element meaning 'be scattered'. The fact that Warlpiri can now be used to discuss central concepts of nuclear physics is clear testimony to the adaptability of Aboriginal languages.

A last word

Linguists would love to have primitive languages to study in order to understand how human language has evolved. But, as I hope to have shown, Aboriginal languages certainly do not fit the bill – in fact, their complexities have played an important role in linguistics over the last three decades in extending our notions of what complex organizing principles can be found in human languages.

Answers

1. *bangaa dangkaya kurrija, bangaa kurrija dangkaya, dangkaya bangaa kurrija, dangkaya kurrija bangaa, kurrija bangaa dangkaya, kurrija dangkaya bangaa*
2. *thengatye*

Sources and further reading

Good introductory books on Aboriginal languages are *Language and Culture in Aboriginal Australia* (Canberra: Aboriginal Studies Press, 1993), Colin Yallop & Michael Walsh (eds.), Colin Yallop's *Australian Aboriginal Languages* (London: André Deutsch, 1982); more advanced but still readable is Robert M. W. Dixon, *The Languages of Australia* (Cambridge: Cambridge University Press, 1980); these books have many onward references. *Macquarie Aboriginal Words* (1994), Bill McGregor and Nick Thieberger (eds.), contains sample vocabularies for a number of Aboriginal languages and pointers to more complete dictionaries. Kayardild examples are taken from the *Kayardild Dictionary and Ethnothesaurus* (Melbourne: University of Melbourne, Department of Linguistics, 1992) and the Kunwinjku examples from a dictionary of Eastern Kunwinjku being prepared by Murray Garde. You might also like to check out the world's first fully formatted hypertext dictionary produced by Peter Austin and David Nathan of

the New South Wales language Gamilaraay, on:
http://coombs.anu.edu.au:8o/WWWVLPages/AborigPages/LANG/
GAMDICT/GAMF_ME.HTM

MYTH 20

Everyone Has an Accent Except Me

John H. Esling

'I don't have an accent!' wails the friend indignantly. And we are all amused because the pronunciation of the utterance itself demonstrates to our ears that the claim is false. The speaker who voices this common refrain believes absolutely that his or her speech is devoid of any distinguishing characteristics that set it apart from the speech of those around them. We listeners who hear it are for our part equally convinced that the speaker's accent differs in some significant respect from our own. The key to understanding this difference of opinion is not so much in the differences in speech sounds that the speakers use but in the nature of 'own-ness' – what does it mean to be 'one of us' and to sound like it? It all comes down to a question of belonging. Accent defines and communicates who we are. Accent is the map which listeners perceive through their ears rather than through their eyes to 'read' where the speaker was born and raised, what gender they are, how old they are, where they might have moved during their life, where they went to school, what occupation they have taken up, and even how short or tall they are, how much they might weigh, or whether they are feeling well or ill at the moment.

The fact is that everyone has an accent. It tells other people who we are because it reflects the places we have been and the things we have done. But the construct of accent, like so many other things, is relative. We may only realize that others think we have an accent when we leave the place we came from and find ourselves among people who share a different background from our own, or when a newcomer to our local area stands out as having a distinctly different pronunciation from most of those in our group – that is, relative to us. The closer we are to our native place and the more people that are there who grew up like us, the more likely we are to sound like those people when we talk. In other words, we share their local accent.

Some countries have one accent which is accepted as 'standard' and which enjoys higher social prestige than any other. This is true of RP (Received Pronunciation) in the UK, of standard French in France and of many countries that have evolved a broadcast standard for radio and television. We may feel that this national standard is accentless and that non-standard speakers, by contrast, have accents. Nevertheless, it has to be recognized that standards that have evolved in the broadcast industry have their roots in language varieties that already exist in distinct social groups and their institutions. To use one particular group's accent in broadcasting is to give that accent a wider reach than perhaps it had before, but the accent itself is no 'less' of an accent than any other, although it may represent groups and institutions with more political and economic power than groups whose members use another accent.

Our perceptions and production of speech also change with time. If we were to leave our native place for an extended period, our perception that the new accents around us were strange would only be temporary. Gradually, depending on our age, what job we are doing and how many different sorts of folks with different types of accents surround us, we will lose the sense that others have an accent and we will begin to fit in – to accommodate our speech patterns to the new norm. Not all people do this to the same degree. Some remain intensely proud of their original accent and dialect words, phrases and gestures, while others accommodate rapidly to a new environment by changing, among other things, their speech habits, so that they no longer 'stand out in the crowd'. Whether they do this consciously or not is open to debate and may differ from individual to individual, but like most processes that have to do with language, the change probably happens before we are aware of it and probably couldn't happen if we were.

So when we say, 'I don't have an accent,' we really mean, 'You wouldn't think I had an accent if you knew who I was and knew where I'd been.' It has more to do with acceptance – agreeing to stop listening to the other as 'other' – than with absolute differences in the vowels, consonants or intonation patterns that a speaker uses. At the most basic level, we acknowledge that every individual will always have some speech characteristics that distinguish him or her from everyone else, even in our local community. This is the essence of recognition – we can learn to pick a friend's voice out of the crowd even though we consider everyone in our local crowd to have the same 'accent' compared to outsiders. So what we call accent is relative not only to experience but also to the number of speech features we wish to distinguish at a time.

Human perception is categorical. When it comes to placing an accent, we listen and categorize according to accents we have heard before. We have a hard time placing an accent that we have never heard before, at least until we find out what to associate that accent with. Our experience of perceiving the sounds of human speech is very much a question of 'agreeing' with others to construct certain categories and then to place the sounds that we hear into them. In contemporary constructivist psychology, this process is called the 'co-construction of reality', in which differences can be said not to exist until we construct them. One result of these principles is that we can become quite attuned to stereotypical accents that we have heard only occasionally and don't know very well, while we become 'insensitive' to the common accents we hear all around us every day. The speech of our colleagues seems 'normal' to our ears, while the speech of a stranger stands out as different from that norm. So we feel that we don't have an accent because of the weight of experience that tells us that we are the best possible example of the 'norm'.

Details of pronunciation conjure up stereotypes. A few consonants and vowels or the briefest of intonation melodies cause us to search our memories for a pattern that matches what we have just heard. This is how we place speakers according to dialect or language group. It is also how we predict what the rest of their consonants and vowels and intonational phrasing will be like. Sometimes we are wrong, but usually we make good guesses based on limited evidence, especially if we've heard the accent before. Because we are used to the word order and common expressions of our language, a stranger's exotic pronunciation of a word which we recognize and understand can be catalogued as foreign, and we may ascribe it to one familiar stereotype or another and predict what the speaker's pronunciations of other words will be like. In this way, we see others as having an accent – because we take ourselves as the norm or reference to compare and measure others' speech.

It is interesting for the student of phonetics to observe the various ways in which one person's accent can differ from another's. There are three 'strands' of accent which Professor David Abercrombie of the Department of Linguistics of the University of Edinburgh for many years taught his students to distinguish: the very short consonant and vowel sounds which alternate in rapid succession; the longer waves of rhythmic and melodic groupings, which we call rhythm and intonation; and the longest-term, persistent features that change very little in a given individual's voice, which we call voice quality.

Consonants and vowels are the building blocks of linguistic meaning, and slight changes in their quality inherently carry large differences in meaning, which we detect immediately. *Bought, bat, bet, bait* is a four-way distinction for an English speaker, but may only be a two-way distinction for a Spanish or Japanese speaker. Differences in vowels can make dialects of English incomprehensible even to each other at first. An American pronunciation of 'John' can sound like 'Jan' to a Scot; and a Scots pronunciation of 'John' can sound like 'Joan' to an American. Consonants are also critical in deciding the meaning of a word. The American who asked if she could clear away some 'bottles' was understood by the pub owner in Scotland to have said 'barrels', not only because of the vowel but also because the d-like pronunciation of the t-sound is almost exactly like the d-like pronunciation of the rolled r in Scots. Again, it is the speaker generating the utterance who thinks primarily in terms of meaning and not in terms of the sounds being used to transmit that meaning. It is the hearer who must translate the incoming speech sounds into new, meaningful units (which we usually call words) and who cannot help but notice that the signals coming in are patterned differently from the hearer's own system of speech sounds. Confusion over the meaning of a word can only highlight these differences, making the translation of meaning more difficult and making each participant in the conversation feel that the other has an accent. The impression is therefore mutual.

Another meaningful component of accent is intonation or the 'melody' of speech. Differences in the rises and falls of intonation patterns, and the rhythmic beat that accompanies them, can be as significant as differences in the melodies of tunes that we recognize or in the beat of a waltz compared to a jig. One of the characteristics of the American comedian Richard Prior's ability to switch from 'white talk' to 'black talk' is the control of the height and of the rising and falling of the pitch of the voice. Even more rapid timing of these rises and falls is an indication of languages such as Swedish and languages such as Chinese which have different tones, that is, pitches that distinguish word meanings from each other. Pitch can have the greatest effect on our impression of an accent or on our ability to recognize a voice. Our mood – whether we are excited or angry or sad – can change the sound of our voice, as the tempo of our speech also speeds up or slows down, so that we may sound like a different person.

Voice quality is the ensemble of more or less permanent elements that appear to remain constant in a person's speech. This is how we recognize a friend's voice on the telephone even if they only utter a syllable. Some voices are nasal; others low and resonant; others breathy; and still others higher pitched and squeaky. Presumably, the better we know a person, the less we feel they have a noticeable accent. Naturally, however, if they didn't have a distinguishable ensemble of accent features, we couldn't tell their voice apart from other people's. Travelers to a foreign country often experience an inability to tell individual speakers of a foreign language apart. As it once did in our native language, this ability comes with practice, that is, with exposure. The reason is that we need time to distinguish, first, to which strand of accent each particular speech gesture belongs and, second, which speech details are common to most speakers of that language and which belong only to the individual. Unless the individual's speech stands out in some remarkable way, we are likely to perceive the collection of common, group traits first.

Much of our perception of accent could actually be visual. Hand and facial gestures which accompany speech could cue a listener that the speaker comes from a different place, so that we expect the person to sound different from our norm. If we expect to hear an accent, we probably will. Sooner or later, wherever they live, most people encounter someone from another place. A stranger from out of town, a foreigner, even a person who had moved away and returned. But even in the same community, people from different social groups or of different ages can be distinguished on the basis of their speech. One of the intriguing linguistic aspects of police work is to locate and identify suspects on the basis of their accent. Often, this technique comes down to the skill of being able to notice details of speech that other observers overlook. Sometimes, an academic approach such as broadcasting a voice to a large number of 'judges' over the radio or on television is necessitated. In this case, an anonymous suspect can often be narrowed down as coming from a particular area or even identified outright. Computer programs are also having moderate success at verifying individual speakers on the basis of their accent. These techniques are sometimes called 'voiceprints', implying that each individual is unique, but as with human listeners, success may depend on how much speech from the individual can be heard and in how many contexts.

One of the most popular characterizations of the notion of accent modification has been George Bernard Shaw's *Pygmalion*, revived on stage and screen as *My Fair Lady*. The phonetician, Professor Higgins, is renowned for tracing the course of people's lives from their accents, and Eliza Doolittle, at the opposite extreme, while probably aware of different accents and able to identify them to some degree, appears at first quite unable to produce speech in anything other than her local-dialect accent. The transformation of Eliza, explained in socio-linguistic terms, is the apparent result of her accommodation to a new social milieu and her acceptance of a new role for herself. In terms of constructivist psychology, she co-constructed a new reality – a new story – for her life and left the old story behind. The transformation had its physical effect (she was no longer recognized in her former neighborhood) as well as its linguistic realization (her accent changed to suit her new surroundings). We all leave parts of the speaking style of our early years behind, while we adopt new patterns more suited to our later years. Whether we change a lot or a little depends on individual choices within a web of social circumstance.

Sources and further reading

The play, *Pygmalion* (New York: Penguin Books, 1951), by George Bernard Shaw is well worth reading and rereading. Failing that, a viewing of the video of *My Fair Lady* provides a tongue-in-cheek (perhaps literally) spoof of both undersensitivity and oversensitivity to accent. *The Encyclopedia of Language and Linguistics* (Oxford: Pergamon Press, 1994) contains a wealth of information on accent, pronunciation and the components of speech that make up accent. The entry on 'Accent' by J. M. Y. Simpson is particularly useful. For more details on one of the most famous of all local accents, see Dennis Preston's chapter on American Speech.

America is Ruining the
English Language

John Algeo

America is ruining the English language – everyone knows that. We have heard it from early days right up to the present. We have heard it from English men and English women, of course, but from Americans as well – self-confessed linguistic vandals. We have heard it from the famous and the obscure. So it must be true. But in what does the ruination lie? How are Americans ruining English?

In the early days, British travelers in the American colonies often commented on the 'purity' of the English spoken in the new world. It wasn't until the American impertinence of 1776 that Americans seem to have begun ruining English. Yet, as early as 1735, a British traveler in Georgia, Francis Moore, described the town of Savannah: 'It is about a mile and a quarter in circumference; it stands upon the flat of a hill, the bank of the river (which they in barbarous English call a bluff) is steep.' The Americans had taken an adjective of nautical and perhaps Dutch origin, meaning 'broad, flat and steep', to use as a noun for the sort of river bank that hardly existed in England and for which, consequently, earlier English had no name.

In 1995, in much the same vein as the comment 260 years earlier, His Royal Highness the Prince of Wales was reported by *The Times* as complaining to a British Council audience that American English is 'very corrupting'. Particularly, he bemoaned the fact that 'people tend to invent all sorts of nouns and verbs and make words that shouldn't be.' By this time the barbarous use of *bluff* for a steep bank had been civilized by being adopted into the usage of the motherland, but doubtless if the Prince had lived about nine generations earlier, he would have agreed with Francis Moore that *bluff* was a word that shouldn't be.

The Prince concluded: 'We must act now to insure that English – and that, to my way of thinking, means English English – maintains its position as the world language well into the next century.' His concern seems to be as much commercial as merely ethnocentrically aesthetic, the English language being one of England's most popular exports, along with gossip about the escapades of the Royals. The Prince, after all, was only doing his bit to keep the English pecker up.

One way Americans are ruining English is by changing it. Many of us, like Francis Moore and Prince Charles, regard what is foreign to us as barbarous and corrupt. We owe the term *barbarous* to the Greeks; they pitied the poor foreigner who could only stammer 'bar-bar' and hence was a 'barbaros'. Barbarians are simply those who do not talk as we do, whether they are outsiders, Yanks or fellow countrymen and countrywomen whose style we do not admire.

The journalist Edwin Newman is a linguistic prophet who sees the language style of his fellow Americans as deadly. In 1974 he vaticinated in a book called *Strictly Speaking*, which was subtitled *Will America be the Death of English?* In it, he too objected to the invention of all sorts of nouns and verbs and words that shouldn't be. In particular he objected to verbosity and euphemism as bad style. A number of Americans bemoan the baleful influence of their fellow citizens on the health or integrity of the language, but only a few, like Edwin Newman, have been able to make a career of it.

In England, on the other hand, a perception that America is ruining the language pervades the discourse of the chattering classes. Indeed, a fair number of British intellectuals regard 'new', 'distasteful', and 'American' as synonymous. A knowledgeable British author complained about the supposedly American pronunciation *conTROVersy* and was surprised to hear that the antepenult accent is unknown in the States, being a recent British innovation. The assumption is that anything new is American and thus objectionable on double grounds.

Change in language is, however, inevitable, just as it is in all other aspects of reality. Particular changes will be, in the eyes of one observer or another, improvements or degenerations. But judgments of what is beautiful or ugly, valuable or useless, barbarous or elegant, corrupting or improving are highly personal and idiosyncratic ones.

There are no objective criteria for judging worth in language, no linguistic Tables of the Law, no archetypical authority called 'The Dictionary', though there are wannabe authoritarians aplenty.

On the other hand, no one is required to like all or any particular changes. It is, in the great Anglo-American tradition, our God-given right to have our own opinions and to take it or leave it when it comes to style in couture, diet, entertainment, religion and language. We need not be equally enthusiastic about catsuits and muu-muus, macrobiotics and *haute cuisine*, grunge rock and Philip Glass, the World Wide Web and MTV, *bank* and *bluff*, or *conTROVersy* and *CONtroversy*. We don't have to like particular changes, or even the fact of change itself. But a language or anything else that does not change is dead.

The eighteenth-century hope that a language could be 'fixed' – that is, improved, or changed in a way some self-appointed linguistic judge would approve of until it reached a state of perfection and then preserved so that it would not thereafter degenerate or change in a way the judge disliked – was a chimera. It was an illusion based on misunderstandings about the nature of language, values and human nature.

The earliest English we can catch sight of in manuscripts of the seventh century was the product of millennia of change. We can only reconstruct its earlier history back through stages we call Anglo-Frisian, Germanic, Indo-European and maybe even Nostratic and Proto-World. During the recorded history of English, the language has changed from something quite incomprehensible to a present-day English speaker, which we call Old English (Hwæt! We Gar-dena in geordagum theodcyninge thrym gehyrdon) to something equally incomprehensible to many of us, computerspeak (Some memory resident programs steal too much of the CPU to work with an asynchronous download).

During its roughly thirteen centuries of recorded history, English has diversified in many ways. Any two varieties of a language become increasingly different from each other when their speakers do not communicate with one other but more alike as those who use them talk among themselves. That is the way language works.

British and American started to become different when English speakers first set foot on American soil because the colonists found new things to talk about and also because they ceased to talk regularly with the people back home. The colonists changed English in their own unique way, but at the same time speakers in England were changing the language too, only in a different way from that of the colonists. As a result, over time the two varieties became increasingly different, not so radically different that they amounted to different languages, as Italian and French had become a millennium earlier, but different enough to notice.

The differences between American and British are not due to Americans changing from a British standard. American is not corrupt British plus barbarisms. Rather, both American and British evolved in different ways from a common sixteenth-century ancestral standard. Present-day British is no closer to that earlier form than present-day American is. Indeed, in some ways present-day American is more conservative, that is, closer to the common original standard than is present-day British.

Some examples of American conservatism versus British innovation are these: Americans generally retain the r-sound in words like *more* and *mother*, whereas the British have lost it. Americans generally retain the 'flat a' of *cat* in *path, calf, class*, whereas the British have replaced it with the 'broad a' of *father*. Americans retain a secondary stress on the second syllable from the end of words like *secretary* and *dictionary*, whereas the British have lost both the stress and often the vowel, reducing the words to three syllables, 'secret'ry'. Americans retain an old use of the verb *guess* to mean 'think' or 'suppose' (as in Geoffrey Chaucer's catch-phrase 'I gesse'). Americans retain the past participle form *gotten* beside *got*, whereas the British have lost the former. (The British often suppose that Americans use only *gotten*; in fact they use both, but with different meanings: 'I've got a cold' = 'I have a cold' and 'I've gotten a cold' = 'I've caught a cold'). Americans have retained use of the subjunctive in what grammarians call 'mandative' expressions: 'They insisted that he leave,' whereas the British substituted for it other forms, such as 'that he should leave' or 'that he left'.

On the other hand, the British are more conservative than Americans in other ways. Thus they continue to distinguish *atom* (with a t-sound) and *Adam* (with a d-sound), whereas Americans typically pronounce the two words alike, with a flap sound that is more d than t like. Similarly, in standard British *callous* and *Alice* do not rhyme, whereas they usually do in standard American, both having a schwa. So too, the British have different stressed vowels in *father* and *fodder*, whereas Americans pronounce those words with the same first vowel. The British have retained an old use of *reckon* in the sense 'think' or 'suppose' in serious discourse, whereas that use in America is old-fashioned or rural, a comic marker of 'hick' talk. The British have retained the term *fortnight*, whereas Americans have lost it. The British have retained the primary meaning of *corn* as 'grain', whereas Americans have changed it to 'maize' (the image many Americans have of 'Ruth amid the alien corn' being both anachronistic and ectopic). The British have retained the inversion of *have* with its subject in questions: 'Have you the time?' whereas Americans use the auxiliary verb *do* with it: 'Do you have the time?'

On balance, it is hard to say which variety of English, American or British, is the more conservative and which the more innovative. A lot depends on how you look at the question. It is clear that the British are keen on (Americans would say 'fond of') the pluperfect, whereas Americans prefer the simple past: British 'He had left before they arrived' versus typical American 'He left before they arrived.' But it is less clear which usage should be regarded as older. Is the American preference a degeneration of the tense system? Or a preservation of the English of the Anglo-Saxons, who had little truck with complex tenses?

Both American and British have changed and go on changing today. Among recent innovations in British English, in addition to the pronunciation of *controversy* already cited, are such vocabulary novelties as *gazumping* and *gazundering*, *Essex man* and *Estuary English*, *toy boy*, and *redundancy* for 'sacking' or 'firing' (a bureaucratic euphemism fit to exercise the spleen of a British Edwin Newman). Paralleling the American retention of the mandative subjunctive ('They insisted that he leave') is a British innovative use of the indicative in such expressions: 'They insisted that he left,' which in American use could only be a statement of fact ('They insisted it was a fact that he had left').

British speakers have also been extraordinarily fertile in expanding the range of use for tag questions. Tag questions are little bobs at the end of sentences that can turn them into questions, or sometimes into something else. The basic tag questions are general English, shared by British and American:

informational: 'You don't wear glasses, do you? (I'm not sure, but think you don't. Am I right?)

inclusive: 'It's a nice day, isn't it?' (It obviously is – I'm not really asking, but just making polite remarks so you can join in the conversation.)

emphasizing: 'I made a bad mistake, didn't I?' (This is a soliloquy. I'm not talking to anybody but myself and don't expect an answer to the rhetorical question. It's the verbal equivalent of underlining.)

The last of the above types is more characteristic of British than of American use, but the next two are distinctively British and are relatively recent contributions of British English to the rhetorical inventory of impoliteness:

peremptory: 'Is the tea ready?' 'The water has to boil, doesn't it?' (Everybody knows you can't make tea without boiling hot water, and you can see that the water has not come to a boil yet, so stop bothering me with idiotic questions.)

antagonistic: 'I telephoned you this morning, but you didn't answer.' 'I was in the bath, wasn't I?' (The reason I didn't answer was that I was in the bath, and it was a great annoyance having you phone at that time; if you had any sense and consideration, you would not have called then. [Never mind that the caller could not possibly know all that – I was annoyed at the time and I'm even more annoyed now at what I perceive to be a complaint when I am the one who was put upon.])

Both Americans and the British innovate in English pronunciation, vocabulary and grammar. British people, however, tend to be more aware of American innovations than Americans are of British ones. The cause of that greater awareness may be a keener linguistic sensitivity on the part of the British, or a more insular anxiety and hence irritation about influences from abroad, or the larger number of American speakers and their higher prominence in fields that require innovation, or perhaps the fact that present-day Americans have cultural rootlets all over the world and so are less aware of the British Isles.

Perhaps Americans do innovate more; after all, there are four to five times as many English speakers in the United States as in the United Kingdom. So one might expect, on the basis of population size alone, four to five times as much innovation in American English. Moreover, Americans have been disproportionately active in certain technological fields, such as computer systems, that are hotbeds of lexical innovation.

It is curious and remarkable that the present state of affairs was foreseen with great accuracy by John Adams, who in 1780, even before it was obvious that the American Revolution would succeed, wrote:

English is destined to be in the next and succeeding centuries more generally the language of the world than Latin was in the last or French is in the present age. The reason of this is obvious, because the increasing population in America, and their universal connection and correspondence with all nations will, aided by the influence of England in the world, whether great or small, force their language into general use.

So is America ruining the English language? Certainly, if you believe that extending the language to new uses and new speakers ruins it. Certainly, if you believe that change is ruin. Certainly, if what John Adams foresaw was ruination.

Index

Index

pleasantness of speech 85–93, 147
Polish 50
polysynthetic 162
prefix 78
present 80, 98
Press-Herald (Lexington) 70
Prince of Wales 176–7
Prior, Richard 173
Private Eye 117–8
pronoun 77, 165
  dual 83, 162
  inclusive 83, 165
  harmonic 163
  interrogative 137
  personal 132–8, 162
  relative 95
  second person 52
  trial 83
Pulp Fiction 125
Pygmalion 174
Python, Monty 125

quantifier, universal and existential
  114–15

racism 64, 106
Ralegh, Sir Walter 66
reckon 180
related languages 50, 58, 160
rhythm 154, 172
Rivarol, Antoine de 23–4, 26, 28,
  30
Romansh 11–12
RP (Received Pronunciation) 170
rules
  of grammar 16, 77, 83, 96–8,
   108
  of usage 51–2
  written *v.* spoken 64
Russian 12, 50, 52, 110, 120, 154, 161

Saturday Night Live 125
schwa 37, 180
Scotsman 18
scripts 33, 53
security, linguistic 142
self-hatred, linguistic 87
sex *see* gender
sexism 43, 64
Shakespeare, William 16, 64, 66–76,
  98, 120, 134
Shaw, George Bernard 174
Shipley, Jenny 45
Sidney, Sir Philip 68
silent letters 35, 38, 53
Slavic languages 50
slovenliness 86, 100–1
social class 64, 87, 88, 99
social confidence 47
social connotations 88, 92
solidarity 147
South Africa 54
Spanish 29, 88, 91, 109, 120, 154, 155,
  172
speaking rate *v.* articulation rate
  151
speed of articulation 145, 150–8, 173
spelling 32–40, 52–3, 58, 61–2
standard variety/language 29, 63–4,
  75, 87, 92, 95, 96, 100, 108, 140,
  170
status 44–5, 75, 88, 90, 99
stereotyping 29, 85, 91, 145, 148, 171
Stevenson, Adlai 21
stress-timing *v.* syllable-timing 154
style 95, 135
subject 80, 97–8, 132, 135, 161
subject complement 133
subjunctive 179, 180
suffix 78
Swedish 39, 50, 52, 54, 173

Index